TWO LECTURES

ON

INTEMPERANCE.

I. — THE EFFECTS OF INTEMPERANCE ON THE POOR AND IGNORANT.

II. — THE EFFECTS OF INTEMPERANCE ON THE RICH AND EDUCATED.

BY HORACE MANN,

THE FIRST SECRETARY OF THE MASSACHUSETTS BOARD OF EDUCATION.

SYRACUSE:

HALL, MILLS, AND COMPANY.

BOSTON: W. J. REYNOLDS & CO.

1852.

STEREOTYPED AT THE
BOSTON STEREOTYPE FOUNDRY.
GEO. C. RAND, PRINTER, CORNHILL.

PUBLISHERS' NOTICE.

The First of the following Lectures was published several years ago, and has long been out of print. The Second was delivered last winter, in Metropolitan Hall in the city of New York, at Syracuse, Rochester, and elsewhere in the state, during the excited struggle in the legislature for and against the "Maine Law," so called. The effort to pass the Maine Law will doubtless be renewed at the ensuing session of the New York legislature, and the friends of Temperance have thought that the publication of these Lectures may serve to promote so beneficent and world-renovating an object.

Syracuse, N. Y., *September*, 1852.

LECTURE I.

THE EFFECTS OF INTEMPERANCE ON THE POOR AND IGNORANT.

IN that most impressive passage of all the Savior's teachings, contained in the twenty-fifth chapter of Matthew, he presents a test of human virtues and vices, and establishes a condition of reward and punishment. He prefigures himself as descending from heaven, and as sitting upon a throne of glory. Holy angels are attendant upon him. Past ages give up their countless dead, now summoned into his presence. You and I, too, my hearers, must be there, — not as idle observers of a wondrous spectacle, but as parties having an infinite interest in the glories or the catastrophes of the scene. Suddenly a voice commands, and the mighty multitude is separated to the right hand and to the left. Above the former are golden portals, opening into realms of bliss. Around the latter, clouds and the blackness of darkness premonish an unspeakable doom. And whether any one may deem this detail of circumstances to be literal or allegorical, the mighty moral is the same.

And what is the criterion on which the Savior makes this infinite difference in results to depend? Is it that of birth, or affluence, or worldly celebrity, or temporal power? Are the high-born, the opulent, the founders of political or intellectual dynasties, the disciples of this or that party or school, conquerors, priests, and prelates, — are these alone found on the right hand; while the poor and the ignorant, the outlawed serf and slave, are ranged upon the left? Is the one party composed of conformists, and the other of non-conformists, to some government standard of truth or faith? No! The sacred record contains no intimation like this. Every thing is made to depend upon good deeds originating in good motives; or upon a bad life emanating from a selfish heart. The instances put are such as every child can understand. The Hottentots in their kraal may know them, as well as philosophers in their lecture room. Did you feed the hungry; did you give to the thirsty the waters of health, and not the waters of destruction; did you clothe the naked; did you visit the sick; did you seek out the prisoner in the solitude of his confinement, to comfort him if innocent, to reform him if guilty? Ah! in the delineation of that august scene, attended by cherubim and seraphim, no topics of vexed philosophy, or of polemical theology, are introduced; but these few and simple questions, level to the capacity of a child, are made the tests of character. In all the cases enumerated, the poor, the homeless, and even the offending, are introduced as the objects of virtuous benevolence or of criminal neglect.

I do not, however, suppose this enumeration to be exclusive, but only illustrative. It gives the most beautiful examples of the virtues, though it does not complete their circle; and we learn the importance of the duties referred to, from their being selected as specimens. An equitable interpretation or construction would doubtless include all kindred duties, and condemn all kindred vices. Emphatically would it include whatever directly or indirectly tends to increase or to diminish the evils of poverty, homelessness, and crime. I think, therefore, that we have the most direct and positive authority of the Savior for saying, that when we are engaged in staying the ravages of Intemperance, we are, in a high and peculiar sense, doing a work commended and commanded by him. I believe this, because, among all the gigantic vices and calamities that have ever scourged mankind, this vice of intemperance is super-gigantic and calamitous.

Among the remarkable features in the account to which I have referred, the most remarkable of them all is Christ's identification of himself with the sufferer, in each case he particularizes. He feels so deep a personal interest in all their sorrows and their privations, as to declare *himself* to have been the victim. It was *I*, he says, who was an hungered; it was *I* who was thirsty; it was *I* who was a stranger; it was *I* who was naked; it was *I* who was sick; it was *I* who was in prison. When you were feasting upon the richest viands, and quaffing the costliest beverages from the wine cup, I was famishing of hunger and of thirst, in the neighboring street or in the neighboring hovel, within the sound of your revelries. When you barred your doors against me, with all your suites of richly-furnished apartments vacant, I had not where to lay my head. When your wardrobes were filled with superfluous apparel, when you profusely squandered the means and appliances of health and ease, I was naked and sick, and laid me down, in friendlessness and solitude, to die. When misfortune and imprisonment befell me, you roamed the world in freedom, but brought no ransom for my body, nor consolation for my spirit. Surely, in all the other records of mankind, whether real or romantic, there is no pathos like this. Religion has had its martyrs; nations their self-immolating patriots; maternal affection has bled out its heart for its offspring; even private friendship has sometimes sacrificed itself for an earthly friend; but where else can be found this union, this oneness, this identification of feeling, with all the distressed and the sorrowing, of all countries and of all centuries, of all the regions of the earth, and of all the generations of men? I say, then, that in chaining down the fiend of intemperance, that he may no longer spread devastation over the earth, we are not only doing a work commanded *by* the Savior, but, according to that beautiful identification, by which he puts himself in the place of the sufferer, we are doing it *for* him and *to* him. To the eye of the Christian, Christ is personally present with all the lost children of the earth; and his true disciples have closer and more intimate communion with him, when they succor the poor, the friendless, the degraded, and the criminal, than when they minister in his temple, or sit around his altar. In checking any form of suffering or of wrong, they pour ointment more precious than that of Mary upon his head, — ointment, whose perfume fills, not only the house, but the heavens.

My object, on the present occasion, is to show the relations of intemperance to the poor and the ignorant, and to those who fall into crime, through the temptations of poverty and ignorance.

I know it may be said that, in my public addresses, I should restrict myself to the subject of education, or at least to topics allied and kindred to it.* It may be averred that, however deeply I may sympathize with those great reformatory movements which characterize our age, I am bound not to awaken jealousies, or inflame hostility, by any direct or indirect interference in behalf of any one of them; but, by a development of the intellect, by a training of the conscience and the formation of exemplary habits, to aim at more broad and general results in establishing the great principles on which they all depend. I acknowledge, to no inconsiderable extent, the justness of this view.

* This Lecture was delivered while its author was Secretary of the Massachusetts Board of Education.

But while I admit its applicability to many, if not most of the benevolent enterprises of the age, there are powerful reasons which seem to me to make the subject of temperance an exception to the rule. In the march of universal improvement, education must lead the van; but, in certain passages of this march, temperance must be the pioneer of education. On human beings as nature leaves them, education can do a transforming work; but, on human beings as intemperance leaves them, education falls as fruitless as water upon flint. Before education can prosper, there must be a desire of improvement and of knowledge; the intemperate man hates both, and stifles the love of them in his children. Before education can prevail, the natural appetites of hunger and thirst must be satisfied; the intemperate man, who has no resource but his labor, experiments upon his children to find the minimum of possible subsistence. No child can learn while half naked and shivering with the cold; the intemperate man not only burns his own vitals, but takes the raiment of wife and children to kindle and to feed the flame. The acquisition of knowledge requires books and apparatus; the intemperate man wears deeper and deeper his crooked path to the dram shop, but he can never find his way to the book store. Education demands and supposes school time; the intemperate man, whenever he can find an infamous purchaser, sells his children to labor, through all their years of nonage, and converts their immortal capacities of usefulness and enjoyment into part and parcel of the wheel-work of a mill. Intemperance is a upas tree planted in the field of education; and before education can flourish, this tree must be cut down. Were all the inhabitants of a village to become intemperate, a schoolhouse would remove from it, of itself.

To the *Poor*, — the destitute, the ill clothed, and the half sheltered, — to those, also, who have never enjoyed the blessings of a good education themselves, and who are sending their own children into the world, with no lamp of knowledge to guide their feet, — to those whose lot is so much more severe than the general lot of mankind, — to them, with a heart full of regard, and with the deepest sympathy for their fortunes, I wish to address a few considerations.

I do not speak here so much of mere almshouse paupers as of those who are one step removed from this degree of destitution. The boundary lines which include the class I refer to may be drawn with sufficient distinctness. If we exclude all those who have added actual guilt to their misfortunes, and who are therefore expiating their offences in the gloom and solitude of a prison; if we exclude, also, all those who, having consumed their own resources, have at length cast themselves upon public charity, there will still remain a large class who are out of the receptacles of poverty and crime, on the one hand, and, on the other, are below the line of comfort and competence, and so are pinched and straitened in all their circumstances, and thwarted in all their plans for improvement; a class whose shoulders are always loaded with a burden which it is galling to bear.

These lines of demarcation embrace a wide and populous region. Its inhabitants suffer in their health through an insufficiency of wholesome and nutritious food. They suffer in their persons, because they cannot get ready for the seasons as they revolve. They suffer in their feelings, because they are hourly conscious of not being treated with the respect which they see accorded to others, who are not better, but only more fortunate, than themselves. They suffer in their minds because they are ignorant, or, what is worse than ignorance, they are a little instructed only upon one side of all the great questions of life, and because they cannot command the common means of intelligence. They suffer in their manners and habits, because through the pressure of outward circumstances they have become less observant of the common decencies and proprieties of life, and because they are debarred from associating with persons of elevated and refined feelings. They suffer often and most unjustly in the estimation of others, because they are obliged to do a thousand things, and to omit a thousand things, which can only be justified by the necessities of their condition, and these necessities they cannot explain. They all suffer in the noblest capacities of their nature,—in their moral and religious sentiments,—because they have fewer restraints from vice, and fewer incentives to virtue, than other men. This class is entirely surrounded, its whole mass is penetrated, by these adverse influences. Whatever the laws of the land may declare, whatever the profounder and juster laws of nature may ordain, the members of this class feel that they do not stand upon the same platform as other men. This truth is thundered in their ears, and it flashes, vivid as lightning, before their eyes, wherever they are, and wherever they go.

By far the greater portion of all this endurance and privation I believe to be unnecessary and avoidable. The poor suffer hardships which are not of nature's appointment. They bear privations which I cannot believe to be permanently involved in the system of divine Providence. They are out of their place in the social system; fallen from that sphere of dignity and happiness which Heaven has prepared them to occupy, and in which they may yet be reinstated.

Observe, for a moment, the scene of things in which we are placed. Mark the infinite profusion which is spread out around us, and the supremacy of man's intellect, which can make it all subservient to his welfare. See the myriads of beings, whose existence has been given them for his raiment and sustenance. The beasts of the forest yield him their furs; the birds of the land and of the sea, their genial covering; the flocks, their fleece; the cotton plant, its cold-resisting filaments; the worm, its beautiful silk. All these productions are converted by machinery, with comparatively little of human labor, into garments and coverings for his protection. Look at these, and then say whether this is a world in which human nerves should be shrinking, and human beings actually perishing with cold. Has not enough been provided for all, — not only for those whose abounding health makes labor a sport, but for infancy, before its capacities of industry are developed, and for age, after its ability to labor has been exhausted?

Look, again, at the abundance which has been provided for the food of man. The rivers and the great oceans swarm with life that has been created for him; the hills and the valleys fatten their thousand herds; the luxuriant soil, absorbing the rain and the sunshine, gives back its harvests in generous requital; gardens and orchards observe the calendar of the year, and supply its changing seasons with their timely varieties; tropical climes send out the redundancy of their delicious fruits; and into so small a neighborhood has the world been brought by the facilities of intercourse, that if any one spot is visited with barrenness, its wants may be supplied from the superfluities of others. Look at this profusion, and then say whether this is a world where hunger should ever rack the body with pain, or incite the mind to crime.

Look, once more, at the fountains of instruction which are open, and whose waters may be easily made to overflow the land. In

New England, every child is born close by a schoolhouse. In this nursery for the mind, such an education is gratuitously given as will enable him, in after-life, to extend his knowledge as much as he pleases. Books are cheap and abundant; lyceums do or may exist in every village; churches, for public moral and religious instruction, are within the sound of each other's bells. Consider these, and then say whether this is a land where a single native-born citizen should ever be ignorant of the glorious history of his own country, untaught in the sources and reasons of moral obligation, devoid of a knowledge of his relation to his Maker and his duties to his fellowmen, or a stranger to that in which he must eternally possess the deepest interest, — to his own spiritual nature, its powers of good and of evil, and its capacities of happiness and of misery.

Yet, in the midst of all this munificence and prodigality of Heaven, a degree of want and suffering abounds. Thousands and tens of thousands, who in point of property are above the grade of poorhouse inmates, still sit down to too frugal a meal; cannot clothe themselves according to the exigencies of the season or the demands of decency; feel unable to incur the expense of instructive books or newspapers; are sorely tempted to keep their children from the day school, for the value of their labor, and from the sabbath school, on account of their dress; and are, in some way, or in all ways, forbidden to indulge their desires for innocent recreation or for laudable self-advancement. Nor are such persons scattered here and there with such wide intervals between, that their unwonted fate excites wonder and astonishment. More or less, they are all around us and in the midst of us. But would society remove the causes of impoverishment, which it has hitherto so diligently encouraged, the number of this class would be almost indefinitely diminished, and it would be no burden to give a comfortable support to all the remainder. I admit that, if compared with any other country in the world, these cases are comparatively few; but I am comparing our condition with a desirable and an attainable standard.

If we are to understand Christ as saying that we shall *always* have a class of *poor* on earth, I believe he referred only to a few extraordinary cases of poverty, — to such as may originate from imbecility of mind, from deformity or malconformation of body at birth, from disabling accident, or from some analogous cause. Neither from the terms of the declaration, nor from its context, can I suppose that it requires for its fulfilment either the immense pauper roll of Ireland, or the far less numerous tenants of American almshouses. Almost all these are supernumerary victims; they are proofs of an unnecessary failure in the working of the social machine; they are gratuitous offerings of society to sorrow and shame.

Should any one, in his astonishment, inquire, What fell agents of destruction, what host of strong fiends, let loose upon the earth and suffered to torment it for a season, had been equal to all this havoc of human welfare, had vanquished the beneficent energies of nature, and checked the current of Heaven's bounties where it flowed broadest and deepest over the earth, let him not seek the mighty cause in any vast apparatus of means, organized and operated by supernatural and infernal agencies. The process by which this immense evil is wrought out is as simple as it is fatal and terrible. With the encouragement of society, and under the sanctions of law, some of the most salutary and nutritious products of nature, — the elements of vigorous health and of long life, — are changed by the action of fire into a poison, compared with which the sting of the adder and the venom of the asp are harmless. It is true that, as this poison first flows from the caldron of the distiller, and is transported by sea or overland to the place where it is to be consumed, and is itself to consume not only the consumer, but all around him, its fatal energy is undeveloped. It is as inoffensive as gunpowder before it is touched by a spark, or as the fire-damp of the miner ere the contact of flame buries all around it in undistinguishable ruin. It then holds disease, and shame, and death, and guilt in a powerfully-concentrated but latent form, and quietly awaits the moment when, being received into the human organism, it shall set the blood on fire, and infuriate the soul.

These woes of intemperance concentrate and expend themselves in a peculiar manner upon the poor. Vastly different would be the condition of this class of our fellow-beings, if the attributes of evil which belong to the distiller's work should display themselves equally, at all times and under all circumstances; if the effects of its malignant energy were fairly divided and apportioned amongst all the capitalists, and laborers, and carriers, and venders who are employed in its preparation and distribubution, until its whole resources of woe were by slow degrees exhausted. Suppose, in the morning of life, the health of one distiller to be suddenly wasted away, and the strong reason of another to totter and sink, and the bosom of a third to be invaded by fierce and gloomy passions, until he thirsted for a brother's or a father's blood; suppose one importer of ardent spirits invariably to lose three fourths of the vessels which he employed in the traffic by their foundering at sea, and another to go home, from counting up the gains of a prosperous voyage, to witness the decline of a lovely wife or a beautiful daughter, dying of secret shame, and a third to be stricken down on his own threshold by a son who, in his childhood, had promised to be the pride and support of his declining years; suppose the retailer, when at night he retires to his chamber for rest, should see the image and hear the echo of the thousand-shaped and thousand-voiced misery which his "BUSINESS" during the day had sent round the wide circle of desolation of which he is the centre;—suppose, I say, the retributions for this manufacture and traffic were to fall thus equally and diffusively upon all who are engaged in them, we should then have far less reason to commiserate and succor the poor, upon whose heads is now poured out so large a portion of the weight and fury of the tempest.

Four fifths of all the sufferings endured by the poor are caused, directly or indirectly, by the use of ardent spirits. Such sufferings never come in the course of nature, nor are they any necessary part of the dispensations of Providence. It is true that, in the natural order of events, devastation does sometimes impress deep memorials of its power upon the face of the earth. In tropical climates, an earthquake, in a single hour, has reduced a populous city to a ruin, and converted the theatre of busy life into a stagnant pool. This, however, even in tropical regions, has occurred but a few times since the earliest periods of the world's history. Occasionally, too, a storm will overcome a ship at sea, and hide it forever beneath the waves, or surprise one upon a lee shore, and dash it in pieces like glass. But such a loss may be repaired by the labor of a few men for a few months. A hurricane sometimes sweeps along a narrow strip of country, and prostrates every thing in its path ; yet another spring will obliterate, with its returning verdure, all traces of the desolation. Sometimes, too, a noble spirit, attuned to the finest sensibilities, and formed for greatness and for universal love, occupies such a position in the social system, that some fierce moral shock crushes his intellect at once, and, instead of the beaming eye and the eloquent tongue of genius, there are left only the mindless gaze and the senseless mopings of idiocy. But probably this does not happen to more than one individual in fifty thousand of our race. And even when human life does perish in the throes and paroxysms of nature, the victims are taken away without any change in their moral condition; they are not tortured for years, and then disgustingly sacrificed; they are not debased and corrupted by crime, and then snatched away from all opportunity of earthly repentance. Their friends and families may lament their loss, but not their shame; tears may fall upon their grave, but they are not tears of blood; for years of wickedness were not made the tardy instrument of death. So, too, it has been when the Omnipotent has dealt personally with obdurate offenders, and smitten them with his own arm for unrepented sins. The cities of Sodom and Gomorrah were consumed in one day, and the hosts of Sennacherib perished in a single night. Fire was not rained upon one member of a family, or upon one individual in a circle of friends, after another, while the rest looked on with unavailing sorrow. The angel of death that entered the Assyrian camp did not torture his victims, year after year, with the fever and the madness of the drunkard's thirst, or the remorse of a drunkard's conscience, before he destroyed them. No! It is the accursed fiend of alcohol alone, that spares to torment; that postpones the day of death, to fill with wretchedness the interval of life; that commands the debasement of the worshipper as preliminary to the worship; and dooms its victims to live to all purposes of disgrace and suffering, after they are dead to all of usefulness and honor. Intemperance is the only curse ever known upon earth, which, at one and the same time, assails a man in all his interests, in all his endearing ties and relations, in all his capacities of bliss, and all his susceptibilities of woe. It hews him down on every side; pursues his body in every step, and his mind in every thought; and overwhelms all of present possession and of future hope, in its remorseless and horrible perdition.

All such misfortunes and discouragements descend with tenfold severity upon the poor. The consequences of intemperance, even upon men of princely fortunes, need no coloring to make a human heart shudder. Yet, so far as property is concerned, the wealthy can afford to be *brutes;* but to obtain prosperity and comfort, the poor must be *men.* And why should any one think this a hard condition? It costs as much, says Dr. Franklin, to maintain a vice, as to bring up two children. He spoke, however, of common vices. The expenses of intemperance would rear a whole family, and give them respectability and happiness into the bargain. A poor man is subjected to continual losses and embarrassments, of which a man in competent circumstances knows nothing. He cannot seize the favorable occasions, nor avail himself of opportune facilities, like the rest of mankind. In regard to the performance of labor and the acquisition of property, there is as much difference between the poor man and his well-conditioned neighbor, as between the artisans and mechanics of a century ago and the craftsmen of the present day. One must lift all his weights with his arms, while the other lifts them by machinery. The hands of one must do his work; the other makes wind, water, and steam perform ninety-nine hundredths of his. If I could have waited until the end of the year for my pay, says the day laborer, I could have had constant employment. If I had possessed an appropriate set of tools, says the journeyman, that profitable job would have been mine. If my credit had been so good that I could have hired men, or purchased teams and wagons, I should have commanded such a lucrative contract. Had I owned stock for such a piece of work, I should have been employed to make it. And so it is through the whole catalogue of opportunities. If a man without means endeavors to carry on any considerable work, he is obliged to mortgage himself to so many men, that it is scarcely possible for him to escape foreclosure. There is, indeed, such a variety of causes and circumstances that maim and cripple a poor man, that the fact of his being poor is, in this country, the best possible excuse for his remaining so. The Hebrew sage utters no more pithy proverb than when he says, the destruction of the poor is their poverty. A tippler pays a barber six or seven dollars a year, in fourpences, because the retailer never allows him to get a dollar ahead to buy a razor. Bodily health, a clear, quick mind, and that good reputation which is universally won by an exemplary life, are the poor man's stock in trade. This stock he is bound to keep sacred by every motive of interest and of duty; how is it that he ever feels at liberty to squander away this, his only capital? The strength requisite for daily labor is the natural income or interest of this capital, and this income may be regularly received for thirty or for forty years without diminution. But intemperance not only stops the interest; it also dissipates the principal. The mere price of the drams amounts to an incredibly large sum; but it is the drinking of them, after all, that causes the destruction. Were a man, instead of paying away his money for rum, to fling the price of four or six drams every day to the bottom of the sea, he might still prosper; but when, in addition to throwing away his money, he throws away his time and his strength, his skill and his judgment, his good habits and his good name, he becomes poor indeed. Then, if sickness or accident befalls him; if a change in fashions, or an improvement in machinery, throws him out of employment, what resource has he but to cast himself upon public charity, or to barter all personal independence for ignominious bread? On the other hand, it is consoling to know that good habits, and the health which usually accompanies them, are more than a match for any adverse fortunes that come in the common course of nature. In the end they tire out what is called *bad luck*, and are sure to come off victorious.

Entire abstinence from all intoxicating drinks, as a beverage, would, with its attendant blessings, in the course of a single generation, carry comfort, competence and respectability, with but very few exceptions, into all the dwellings in the land. This is not a matter of probability and conjecture. It depends upon principles as certain and fixed in their operation as those which regulate the rising of the sun or the revolution of the seasons. We may calculate upon such a result with certainty, if there be any fidelity in the laws of nature. Let the poor man look around upon his more fortunate neighbors who began life in the same circumstances as himself; and let him candidly seek the true cause for the present difference between them. He will find an answer in the fact, either that they have enjoyed a better character than himself for intelligence, industry, and trustworthiness, or that they have had sober relations,. from whom they received patronage, assistance, or property. And so, in almost all cases, would comfort and competence have been his fortune, had not every stream of prosperity, as it flowed towards him, been dried up by the distiller's fire.

Again I say, let each individual of this class of unfortunate persons, so many of whom are suffering, not from any fault or vice of their own, but from the faults or vices of others with whom they have been connected, ask himself why it is that he is not able to command the ordinary comforts of life; why it is that he has not a little property laid up beforehand as a resource in sickness or misfortune, or, should he fortunately escape these, then, to leave to his children as a letter of introduction to the world; why he has not the usual means of improving his own mind, and of giving his children the inestimable advantages of a good education; why, in short, he has not a comfortable home to dwell in, decent apparel for himself and his family to go abroad in, a farm in fee simple to cultivate, or some good trade with a complement of tools for carrying it on, books upon his shelves, a right in some social library, and a pew in the meeting house. Any true oracle would give the response in one word, *Intemperance*, either in himself, or in some one with whose fortunes his own were linked!

Or, to be more specific; — I believe that almost every native-born, poor citizen of our community would discover the cause of his poverty in a true answer to one or more of the following questions: —

Should I ever have inherited any property

from any relative, or had it bequeathed to me by any friend, had it not been lost or squandered in consequence of the drinking of intoxicating liquors ?

Have I ever lost any debts due me from intemperate men, who, had they been blessed with sober habits, would have been able to pay me all, besides having a competency left for themselves ?

Have I ever been bound or become surety for other men, who became unable to pay their debts in consequence of drinking, and who, therefore, left those debts for me to pay ?

What amount of taxes have I had to pay for the support of intemperate paupers and their families in poorhouses ; or for the prosecution of drunken offenders in courts of justice, and for their maintenance in jails and prisons ?

What would be the amount of all the money I have expended for intoxicating drinks, had it been saved and kept at interest until the present time ?

Have I ever injured my health by drinking, so as to lose time, or to lessen the value of my labor, or to incur the expenses of sickness ; and what would be the amount of all such losses, with interest, up to the present time ?

Has drinking rendered me less competent to

manage my business, less judicious in my contracts, less skilful in my trade, less able to earn the highest wages, or to offer the best manufactures or products in the market; or have others, who would have employed me or purchased from me, ever acted upon such a belief?

Have I ever, in consequence of drinking, met with any accident in my person or property, which otherwise would not have befallen me; or have I ever, from the same cause, been seduced into gaming, or buying lottery tickets, or tricked into any other foolish bargains?

Have I ever, when in a state of excitement from the same cause, been provoked into a quarrel, or assailed an individual in his person, property, or reputation, for which I have afterwards been compelled to make reparation in damages?

Have I ever lost an agency, or forfeited my chance for a profitable trust, in consequence of habitual or occasional indulgence in liquor?

Have I ever spent time at the dram-shop or tavern, which, had it been devoted to reading and the cultivation of my mind, would have stored it with useful information respecting men and things; would have made my reflections happier when engaged in my ordinary employment, and would have secured more respect and deference for my opinions among neighbors and townsmen? Or, had I devoted the time spent at the dram-shop to teaching my children or encouraging them in their studies, should I not have made them happier and better, and greatly increased their chances of prosperity in life?

In consequence of my appetite for liquor, have I never been regardless of my language, my manners, and my appearance, so as to produce an aversion from mingling in the society of respectable and pure-minded men, or so as to repel such men from seeking association with me; and thus, have I not lost the standing in society which I once held, or been kept back from that which I might otherwise have obtained; and have not my wife and children suffered, in the same way, from my misconduct?

Have I never, in consequence of rashness or passion, occasioned by indulgence in drinking, quarrelled with a friend and lost him, from whose aid and influence in society I might otherwise have derived assistance, employment, and repute?

In consequence of habitual excitement from drink, or the cravings and gnawings of an appetite for it, has not my former control over my temper been lost, my affection for my wife and family alienated or deadened; and have not jealousy, discord and heart-burnings often entered my dwelling, which should have been, and which otherwise would have been, the abode and sanctuary of happiness and peace?

And finally, has the intemperance of my parents or my children, of my husband or my wife, of my brothers or my sisters, ever stripped me of my property, or debarred me from accumulating more, or checked my advancement in the world, or so imbittered all the joys of life that I have been sunk in discouragement or driven to despair, and have sought relief from the anguish of contemplating their ruin by madly braving the same perdition myself?

Now, I appeal confidently to every sensible man's observation, whether these questions do not indicate the true causes of ninety-nine hundredths of all the poverty and the wretchedness known in our land. How many men, commencing life under the auspices of sober habits, have married, and become the happy fathers of happy children; and, for years, have added something every day to the stock of their knowledge, the amount of their property, and the respectability of their good name; when, in the midst of their prosperity, they have become the prey of the spoiler? Suddenly, the process of decomposition begins in all places at once. Bills of sale dispose of their goods. Mortgages and executions seize upon their houses and lands. Health, judgment, reputation, languish for a little while, and die. Their daughters are driven out to service, where their virtues are exposed to contamination, — having no longer the counsels of a mother, who has gone broken-hearted to the grave. Like untimely fruit shaken from the tree, their sons are sent abroad with only a stinted education, and before their principles are formed and confirmed; and, instead of carrying with them an elevation of moral character and sentiment derived from a father's instruction and example, they go with the disheartening consciousness that they bear a dishonored name. And when they arrive at years of manhood, what can be more natural than that some of them, who have been subjected to the most adverse influences, and who are infinitely more to be pitied than blamed, should contemn the knowledge they do not possess, should deride the civility of manners they have never been taught to cultivate, and, having no rational gratification in books or in intelligent society, should seek the excitements of the gaming-house and the dram-shop, and should look, through life, with malign regard upon those civilizing and refining institutions whose necessary effect is to render their inferiority more conspicuous?

This subject is so immensely important that I wish to consider it in the intimate relation which it bears to one of the most important business departments in the community. Directly or indirectly, the grocer or retail dealer supplies the means of intemperance to the great majority of intemperate men. I believe the general opinion has been, and, to some extent, still is, that intemperate men are the grocer's or retailer's most profitable customers. Certainly, in all the efforts which have been made for a reform, whether by means of legal restraint or moral suasion, the grocers and retailers, *as a class*, have arrayed themselves among its opponents. Now, I believe it to be perfectly demonstrable, that they are losers instead of gainers by the traffic they carry on and defend. I believe the profits of their business will be greater, just in proportion as the community becomes more sober. I therefore propose to devote the residue of this Lecture to a consideration of the relation which they bear to the cause of temperance; for, by their coöperation, the number of the poor can be rapidly reduced, while, at the same time, this great blessing will redound more and more to their own pecuniary benefit.

It is obvious that the grocer or retail dealer occupies a very important station in society. The services of other citizens, — of the mason or the housewright, the blacksmith or the whitesmith, the physician or the lawyer, — we seldom need; but we can scarcely have a comfortable meal, unless the grocer furnishes some of its materials. Nor is it for thanksgivings, weddings, or holidays alone, that we ask his permission for our customary enjoyments. Rarely does any respectable family spread a table, morning, noon, or night, which is not supplied with some of the articles of his merchandise. The store-rooms of thriving housekeepers abound in commodities purchased of him; and if the circumstances of any family are so improved that they begin to live more generously and hospitably than before, the grocer knows it sooner than the guest.

The grocer stations himself in the midst of the populous village, or in some conspicuous place on the city streets, and there, by his display of the rich productions of every quarter of the globe, he tempts every man to become a purchaser. While the watchmaker and jeweller expect profits from those only who can wear watches and jewels, the chaise and carriage-maker only from those who keep up such expensive establishments, and the bookseller only from persons of some literary or scientific taste, the grocer expects profits from every body, because every body eats.

But as the articles consumed by different families differ greatly both in quantity and quality, it is obvious there must be a great difference in the profits which the grocer derives from their custom. One man buys a bag of excellent coffee; another, a few pounds of burnt rye or peas. One buys loaves of double refined sugar; another uses molasses, or, perhaps, indulges occasionally in a little well-sanded Havana.

But no prudent man, no true son of New England, ever purchases beyond his ability to pay; and though an improvident man may discard this standard, the seller always has, or certainly always should have, especial reference to it. The natural restriction is on the side of the customer. Every grocer could *sell* ten times as much as he now sells; but, unfortunately for him, his customers have not the ability to buy.

The amount of the grocer's profits, then, depending, not upon his ability to sell, but upon the ability of his customers to buy, it would be no proof of his being either a miser or a Jew, if he should anxiously inquire, *upon what this ability to buy depends.*

In a climate and soil like those of New England, and, indeed, the greater part of the Northern States, where there are neither mineral productions to be dug from the bosom of the earth, nor spontaneous harvests to be reaped from its surface, there are, so far as human agency is concerned, only three primary original sources of wealth.

1. Health, strength, skill, and intelligence.

2. Industry and perseverance in the application of them.

3. Frugality, economy, and sound judgment, in preserving, investing, and managing whatever may have been acquired.

The possession of the above-named qualities enables a man to buy, because they invariably supply him with the means of buying. Is it not too clear for argument, that a hundred healthy, strong, industrious men, with the steady eye, the true hand, and the intelligent mind, will earn more, and therefore be able to expend more, than an equal number of rum-stricken wretches, with trembling hands, tottering limbs, and besotted intellects?

Whatever, then, wastes health, consumes

strength, destroys skill, or substitutes indolent for industrious habits, must necessarily diminish the wealth of the community; and therefore, just as necessarily, subtract from the amount of the grocer's business.

The grocer stands between the producer and the consumer. He is the agent through whose hands exchanges are made of what others have earned. He creates nothing. He adds no intrinsic value to his commodities. He does not turn steel into watch-springs, nor mulberry leaves into silk. He cannot work more hours to make up for a bad day's business. When he has received all that his customers are able to pay, his day's labor is ended, whether the sun has gone down or not. But let others earn more and he receives more, as the river rises when its fountains are more copiously fed.

Though the patronage and profits of all traders depend upon the prosperous or adverse circumstances, the advancing or receding condition, of the community, yet the grocer's thermometer feels the expansion of prosperity or the contraction of adversity earliest and most sensibly. Look at the relation in which he stands to the poorest families amongst us who are out of the poorhouses. Whenever, by good fortune or extra exertion, they get a few shillings, before they go to the carpenter or the mason to get a hovel built or repaired, before they go to the cabinet-maker to procure any article of furniture, before they go to the dry-goods dealer to obtain any materials for clothing, before they pay any rent, or a tax, or the doctor's bill, or a debt of any kind, they go to the grocer to purchase sugar, coffee, tea, molasses, rice, flour, butter, cheese, or articles of a similar kind, if they are temperate; but rum, if they are not. In either case, the grocer knows, better than any other man, what their first acquisitions amount to. And the articles in which the dealing commences generally determines the future character of that dealing. It determines, also, whether they shall ever contribute any thing to encourage and uphold the other classes of traders, or the mechanics, or those who are engaged in any other of the various vocations of mankind. If the substantial aliments of life are called for and supplied, the condition of the family is, for a longer or a shorter period, improved. Having tasted new gratifications, they are encouraged to new exertions; and, in this country, with but few exceptions, nothing but proper *exertion* is required to raise men from poverty, and to surround them at least with all the less expensive comforts of life. A desire to obtain further supplies, I say, is excited. Occasional exertion is matured into a habit of industry. In the mean time, skill is improved. More and better work is done, and in shorter periods. Poverty begins to cast off its old skin. They rise through the gradations of labor, from that which is less, to that which is more lucrative. The mind sympathizes with the body, and takes an upward spring. Thus the very germ of improvement is quickened. The secret source of human happiness is touched; for such is the nature with which divine Providence has endued the race of men, that their greatest good, their highest happiness, depends not so much upon their exemption from positive ill, nor the magnitude of their desirable possessions, nor the lustre of their talents or their wisdom, as it does upon their constant improvement and progression from day to day, — their conscious ascension to a better and a higher state of being. To occupy one point in the scale of being, however elevated, if one must be always stationary there, is far less conducive to human happiness, than to be constantly moving upwards, though along a low point in the scale.

But, on the other hand, if the poor man calls

for and receives ardent spirits, the stimulus of the day becomes the torpidity of the week. Exertion fails. The desire to improve his own condition and that of his family, the desire to educate his children, — in fine, all generous and laudable desires, are swallowed up in the desire *to drink.* He abandons the hope of rising to an equality with his more fortunate neighbors. He and his family remain fixed and stationary, *at the point of bare subsistence.* Who ever knew a laboring man, who, after having earned a little property, and then becoming intemperate, did not grow poorer and poorer, until all was gone? Who ever saw the table spread in the house of such a one, without witnessing, first the irregular appearance, and then the regular absence, of most of those articles of daily sustenance which the grocer furnishes? It is true that some dealer in intoxicating drinks now gets all which chance or fortune puts into his customer's hands. But the whole is far less than a tithe of the gains of regular industry. Besides, as the drunkard never pays any thing, or, at best, but little, to the tailor, shoemaker, hatter, bookseller, &c., &c., none of these persons are enabled to purchase any more of the grocer than if he had never existed. Indeed, they are far less able, for, by and by, with the grocer's assistance, they have to pay all the victim's taxes, to provide a school for his children, if they have any, and to pay for their school books, and often to support him in jail, and his family in the poorhouse. Surely the profit account with such a customer must be now at an end. When the eggs are addled, the prospect for chickens becomes desperate.

But let me examine more minutely the relation of an intemperate and a temperate customer, *as a mere source of gain*, to the grocer who supplies them. Take them from the same condition of life. Suppose them to have been possessed, originally, of equal capacities. Let each be the head of a small family. I make no reference to them here as moral and accountable agents, but propose to compare them with each other, *as mere instruments of gain.* For the present, I leave the *soul* out of the account. Let this being of heavenly workmanship, " so noble in reason, so infinite in faculties, in form and moving so express and admirable, in action so like an angel, in apprehension so like a God," — let him for a moment, I say, be regarded as of no more intrinsic value than if he were " made, after supper, of a cheese-paring." It is not the swift ascension of his immortal nature, through the bright scale of infinite improvement, that I would now contemplate; but only his movements backwards or forwards along a scale graduated simply for the measurement of dollars, dimes, and cents.

There is one fact which can be proved in a thousand ways, namely, that as soon as a man becomes the slave of intemperance, his labors, considering his intervals of idleness, his diminished skill, the subordinate kinds of employment to which he is put, and the mischiefs, voluntary and involuntary, which he is perpetually committing, have not more than one third part the value of those of a temperate man. There are exceptions to this, I acknowledge; but I speak of the average of drunkards and hard drinkers. Taking into view the shortened period of an intemperate man's life, and the fact that, if he lives to advanced age, he is disabled and broken down, I do not believe there is an intelligent farmer or master mechanic, of any kind, who would hire such a man, at the age of twenty, thirty, or forty years, *agreeing to take him for the rest of his life*, and give one sixth part so much for all his future services, as he would for those of a temperate man. Now, pecuniarily considered, the commonwealth stands to these men in the relation of an employer. I will, however, abate but two thirds of the value of his future labor.

Exclusive of Sundays and holidays, there are about three hundred working days in the year. The temperate man will work three hundred days, and earn three hundred dollars. His wife can earn fifty more ; — total, three hundred and fifty dollars. The drunkard earns one third as much, — one hundred dollars. His wife, driven to greater exertion, besides doing all the harder work about the house, from which temperate and kind husbands always relieve their wives, will earn seventy-five dollars ; — total, one hundred and seventy-five dollars.

Temperate man's income, ...		$350.00
Expenses of do. : —		
House rent, ...	$40.00	
Fuel, ...	25.00	
Clothing, ...	50.00	
Butcher's meat, &c., ...	70.00	
Groceries, (*no rum,*)	75.00	
Horse and chaise hire, for health or recreation, hospitable entertainment of friends, little extra articles of dress or furniture, newspapers, books, charity, &c., for all which the drunkard expends nothing, .	60.00	
	$320·00	

Excess of income over expense, or $30 laid by, ...	30.00
	$350.00
Drunkard's income, ...	$175.00
Expenses of do. : —	
House rent, ...	$30.00
Fuel, ...	25.00
Clothing, ...	25.00
Butcher's meat, &c., ...	35.00
Groceries,* (*except rum,*)	20.00
Four drams a day, at three cents each, (or its equivalent in rum bought by the quart or pint,) . .	43.80
	$178.80
Excess of expenses over income; (and singularly fortunate for his neighbors if this is all,)	3.80
	$175.00

It should be remarked generally, that the proportion which these items bear, one to another, must vary considerably in different parts

* I suppose that, generally, the groceries of a good housekeeper would amount to one fourth or one fifth of his annual expenses; but a drunkard can afford but few, at any rate; and when he goes to the store for *necessaries*, rum is so much more necessary than butter, cheese, sugar, tea, coffee, flour, rice, &c., &c., that, in the competition between them, the latter must always yield.

It will be observed that I have not taken the lowest class of cases.

of the country; but the above is believed to approximate to an average. In one section, there may be a departure from exactness in some items of the above estimate; but it may be balanced by a different condition of things in another section. The disposition, too, of the drunkard will vary the mode of his expenses. If he be social and companionable, he will be more of a tavern-haunter, and spend more money there; but if he be a selfish, solitary sot, he will hie away with his bottle to some secret nook or corner, where, in solitude and in darkness, abandoning the companionship and sympathies of men, he will draw closer the bonds which bind him in alliance with devils.

To all this it may be replied, on the part of the grocer, that the profit of a small capital invested in ardent spirits is much greater than that of an equal capital invested in other things. This is undoubtedly true, and, *if the drunkard's money would only hold out*, like that of the sober man, the answer, to one who regards money alone, would be complete. But if the grocer receives one fifth, or about that proportion, of the annual expenditures of a thriving and industrious citizen, each year, then, in every five years, he will receive from each citizen an amount equal to his whole annual expenditure for one year. But supposing for a moment that profits are equal on the different articles of traffic, he must receive a hundred dollars, or any other given sum, from the drunkard, three times every five years, in order to derive the same profit from his whole custom as from that of a temperate man. If the drunkard earns but one third as much as the temperate man, those who deal with him must either make three times the profit from his custom, or they must have that custom three times as often, in order to obtain the same amount in the same time. To a very great extent, however, the fact of higher profits derived from dealing with the drunkard is counterbalanced by the correlative fact of bad debts. In the country, where traders suffer so much less from fluctuations in business, and from the guilt of lottery-like speculation, than they do in cities, almost all bad debts originate with intemperate men. With the exception of their rum debts, this class of men is always very remiss in making payment, and oftentimes debts due from them are not only wholly lost, but money derived from sober men is taken to pay a lawyer's bill, a sheriff's bill, and costs of court. More than four fifths of the insolvent estates settled in the country probate offices are made insolvent by this energetic cause of impoverishment. Upon these a small dividend is sometimes received, and sometimes not. This taking a dividend of *twenty-five per cent.* is as though a farmer should sow a bushel of grain, and, after all his own labor, should harvest from it only a peck.

But the argument has not yet laid hold of its strongest supports. If a grocer be made richer by changing one customer from temperate to intemperate habits, he would be made a hundred fold richer by thus changing the characters of a hundred. Give, then, to a grocer a monopoly of the trade of a hundred families, in common circumstances as to property, for twenty years. In return for this monopoly, however, let him be bound to remain among them for twenty years, to share their fortunes, pay taxes according to his property, &c., &c. Invest him with some despotic power, or some devilish art, by which he can transform them all into drunkards in a week. What will be his condition, I will not say at the end of twenty, but at the end of five years? Even before half this time has elapsed, he will find bad debts multiplying upon his books. If he applies to an attorney for coercive assistance, he will have occasion to *take* receipts for costs paid much oftener than to *give* them for debts collected. His taxes will soon double, treble, quadruple, although the public school will not be kept so long, nor the public roads be so well repaired. His utensils will be borrowed and broken, or never returned. The chaise or wagon he has lent will be overturned and damaged, perhaps destroyed. His oxen and his horses will be lamed, wind-broken, or maltreated. Assaults, batteries, and riots will be committed about his premises, and he will be summoned to court as a witness, and obliged to leave his business for a week. His money drawer will be rifled, and he must prosecute the offender. Some of the neighboring children will become beggars, and extort his property. Others will turn thieves, and purloin it. One of his debtors will move away or abscond; one will die from some debauch, or rum-produced accident; one will break a limb, and be carried to the poorhouse; one will become insane; one commit suicide; one be sentenced to imprisonment, leaving his wife and family upon the town; and another will expiate his offence upon the gallows! What will be the real value of the monopoly of such a set of customers, at the end of twenty years!

But it may be asked, How can all this be without great profits? How can property, once in being, be lost by the intemperate without being gained by the temperate?

The drunkard realizes the fable of the Upas tree. Destruction is all around him. The house in which he lives descends with a swifter decay. The farm he manages forgets to bear the life-sustaining harvest, and is luxuriant only in briers and thorns. Weeds choke out the grass in his fields. Insects consume his orchards. His garden is smitten with barrenness. His fences fall, and lay open his crops to depredation. His cattle become like the "lean kine" of Pharaoh. If he is engaged in trade, his calculations always err. His means prove inadequate to the execution of his plans. He consorts with rogues and sharpers, who defraud him. He seeks to retrieve his fortunes by gaming or buying lottery tickets, and that is only a shorter course to inevitable ruin.* If he be a mechanic, his right hand forgets its cunning. He frames a house whose parts will not go together. If a tailor, he spoils the cloth he would cut into garments. His work, of whatever kind it may be, ceases to be inquired after, and bears the lowest price in the market. In fine, what-

* It has been truly said that the number of persons annually destroyed by lightning is greater than the number of those who draw any considerable prize in a lottery; so that every man who buys a lottery ticket may have the comfortable reflection that, whatever chance he has of drawing a prize, he has a still greater chance of being killed by lightning.

ever the occupation of an intemperate man may be, disaster attends him. His rashness upsets a stage. His negligence explodes a powder-mill or a steamboat. His foolhardiness wrecks a ship. Out of the countless millions of wealth which are every year cast into this ocean, a few dollars may fall upon the shallows or near the shore, and be reclaimed; the rest sinks into unfathomable depths, and is lost forever.

But now let us suppose the grocer or retail dealer to commence business in the midst of only one hundred families of temperate habits, each of them earning from three hundred to six hundred dollars annually. Within these limits, as to income, it is presumed a great majority of the citizens of this state would be found. The average is four hundred and fifty dollars each. Suppose each family to spend only one fifth part of its income for groceries, *rum always excepted.* Each one would then carry to the grocer ninety dollars a year, or the whole of them nine thousand dollars. A net profit of *fifteen per cent.* on this sum would be thirteen hundred and fifty dollars. A profit of ten per cent. would be nine hundred dollars. With the preservation of temperate habits, all would gradually advance in wealth, and be able to live better and spend more; — making use, not only of greater quantities, but of superior qualities of flour, rice, sugar, coffee, tea, &c., with some of the fruits of Italy, France, or the Indies. Each family now becomes tributary to the grocer's prosperity. The streams all run to his reservoir, and yet the fountains are not exhausted, but rise higher and higher. Each one is able to take a newspaper, to purchase a few new and valuable books every year; and, together, they can constantly improve their public schools, and form school district and social libraries. The fathers can settle their sons upon a farm, in business, or in a profession, and give their daughters a dowry in marriage. Peace abounds. Crimes are unknown. The aged descend to the grave with honor. The young rise up, happy in the ability, and more happy in the desire, faithfully to perform their part of the great duties of life. At the end of twenty years, though all would have a competency, and many, what would, in such a place, be called wealth, yet the gains of the grocer would probably be equal to those of any other man. There would be but one house in the village with failing revenues, and exhibiting symptoms of desertion and decay, — the village poorhouse.

In fairness, however, it should be admitted, that there is one combination of circumstances, in which the grocer would enhance his profits by changing the character of his customers. If he had a hundred sober customers, and knew that he should live but two years to trade with them, it must be admitted that he would gain money faster, could he turn them all at once into drunkards; but would a man who knew that he should die at the end of two years do this?

The grocer sustains incalculable loss in another way. In every circle of society, there are constantly rising up a few men, who, from extraordinary enterprise, skill, or talent, soon accumulate large fortunes, and, for the last half of their lives, make his most profitable customers. When such men become intemperate, their tendency to descend is as much stronger than that of other men as was their ability to rise. Great energy resides in them, and it will propel them rapidly one way or the other. To create or foster habits of intemperance in such men is to pursue and exterminate the most active agents of his prosperity. It would be less improvident in the mechanic to break in pieces the most ingeniously wrought tools of his craft, or in the farmer to give his best seed grain to his cattle, or to cut down for fuel the finest fruit trees in his nursery.

There is also an indirect way in which the grocer loses custom and profit, which, I apprehend, has been altogether overlooked. Drunkards will pay for rum when they will pay for nothing else; for the plain reason that they love rum better than they love any thing else. Hence other men are more exposed to *direct* loss from their inability or disinclination to fulfil their engagements than the grocer. But when an insolvent drunkard borrows his neighbor's horse, and kills or disables him; hires his carriage, and destroys it; gets a friend or relative to indorse a note, and leaves him to pay it; borrows money, and never returns it;—in all these cases, those who suffer by him, if they are themselves prudent and thriving men, *will curtail their own expenses*, until they have made up the loss; and the grocer probably suffers more from this curtailment than any other man; because a temporary diminution in the use of his commodities can be borne without any change in the outward style of living; and because high-spirited men will always stint themselves in their private indulgences rather than in those which are open to general observation.

Many of the above remarks have a more

especial reference to the grocers or retail dealers in the country than to those who belong to a city, — especially if the city is a port of entry and a place for the manufacture of alcoholic drinks. There are other views which apply with peculiar force to the residents of cities. Many city grocers, besides supplying a circle of customers around their own doors, furnish country traders with their assortments, and thus become a kind of wholesale dealers. If one grocer in the city supplies, in this way, the commodities sold by ten grocers in the country, every change in their business will be felt by him in a tenfold degree. If they extend or contract their business to the amount of a hundred dollars each, it is an extension or contraction of a thousand dollars to him. To his profits, it is the difference between multiplication and subtraction.

If there be any veracity in experience, one other fact is certainly true, namely, that almost all the losses sustained by city merchants and traders from dealing with country customers, bear the same relation to intemperance that an effect does to its cause. If another drop of ardent spirits never crossed the boundary line of the city to blast the fair fields of the country, the gold and silver of the country would then come to the city purified from almost all its dross.

In fine, there result from intemperance a perpetual havoc and destruction of property already earned, and also of the natural elements and economical practices from which property is created. Both in city and in country, health is prostrated, strength paralyzed, skill deadened, talent extinguished, habits of industry and perseverance annihilated, the lessons of frugality and economy contemned and forgotten, and all the noble capacities of man made to counterwork their natural aptitude to promote his welfare. Were the use of intoxicating drinks, as a beverage, entirely and forever discontinued, the grocer or retail dealer would, of course, lose the difference between the *greater* profits accruing from their sale, and the *smaller* profits accruing from the sale of other commodities; but, in generous requital for this loss, he would receive his customary gains upon the many millions of property, whose very existence depends upon that discontinuance.

With two brief considerations, I will bring this Lecture to a close.

The first pertains to the relation which all the various producing classes in society bear to the manufacturer and the vender of intoxicating drinks. What effect have the importer and seller of alcoholic liquors upon the dry goods dealer, the baker, the butcher, the tailor, the hatter, the shoemaker, the mason, the house builder, the cabinet maker, the upholsterer, the gardener, fruiterer, and farmer, in all their various productions; the bookseller, the newspaper editor, and even upon the watchmaker, the jeweller, the sculptor, painter, or other workmen in the fine or ornamental arts? Is not the business of the former a perpetual blight upon that of all the latter, — worse than excises or monopolies, than taxes or imposts? The vintage, cultivated by the dealer in intoxicating drinks, sucks all the fertility out of the earth, and absorbs all the nourishment out of the atmosphere, for miles around him. At the liquor dealer's approach, nature withers, man mourns, society sickens, civilization countermarches. All men engaged in all other kinds of business whatever, have a common interest to unite in abolishing this kind. They should marshal themselves against it as against a common foe, — as against one whose overthrow is their success, whose destruction is their prosperity, whose triumph is their ruin. Compare, or rather contrast, the pecuniary benefits which tradesmen and mechanics, of every kind, receive from a company of a thousand squalid and destitute immigrants, however much these may *need* for food, clothing, or shelter, with the profits which the same classes would derive from a village of a thousand educated, industrious, and temperate people; and see how deeply all are interested in stopping this prodigious leakage from their common reservoir of gain.

My second and closing remark is, that all political economists, all philanthropists, all moral reformers, and pioneers of human progress, all ethical and religious teachers, whether they lean more to the side of speculation or of practice, are related by the closest moral affinity to temperance reformers; because there will, always and necessarily, be a limit to the successes of the former, until the latter have achieved a universal conquest. Emphatically is this true of all teachers and friends of universal education, and of the spread of Christianity. Temperance must dispossess the demoniac of all his devils, before education and Christianity can take him into their sacred keeping, and become ministers for restoring to his mind the lost image of his Maker.

LECTURE II.

THE EFFECTS OF INTEMPERANCE ON THE RICH AND EDUCATED.

THERE are different classes of truths, belonging to the subject of Temperance, which are respectively applicable to all the different conditions of life.

On a former occasion, I solicited the attention of the Poor and the Ignorant to some considerations deemed particularly applicable to their condition. I trust I succeeded in demonstrating that either their own use of ardent spirits, or, — as it much more frequently happens, — the use by those for whose indulgences they are made to suffer, is the grand procuring cause of their misfortunes and their social inequality. I trust it was proved to the satisfaction of every reflecting mind, that if this one source of poverty and degradation could be dried up, the great majority of the poor would rise to the possession of competence, the ignorant would share in the blessings of knowledge, and both would be delivered from those beguiling temptations which now so often seduce them into dishonor and ruin.

On the present occasion, I solicit the attention of those favored individuals in society who possess a full mediocrity, or more than a mediocrity, of property and of intelligence, and who, therefore, according to the commonly received notions of wealth and of attainment, can be denominated neither poor nor ignorant. As contrasted with the poor and ignorant, this portion of the community may be called Rich and Educated. There is a class of truths on the subject of temperance, vital alike to their pecuniary prosperity and to their social well-being, and bearing with great efficiency upon the character and condition of that society, which they, in common with all other men, must leave as an inheritance to their children. I say, which they, in common with all other men, *must* leave as an inheritance to their children; for, in this respect, no choice is left even to the most affluent or the most powerful. A man may modify, at pleasure, the form in which he will leave his estate to his offspring. He may give to one child houses, to another lands, and to another money, or books, or works of art; or if he will begin early and conduct judiciously, he may, so to speak, *spiritualize* his worldly goods, and bequeath to his children the precious legacy of education instead of the grosser one of gold. But the condition of society, — its upward or its downward tendencies, its probity or its profligacy, — he must leave, whatever it may be. Here he has no option; and when the hour of death comes, he may as well attempt to change the order of the seasons, by a provision in his last will and testament, as to remove the moral dangers or increase the moral guaranties of that state of society to whose tender mercies his children are committed.

I am not about to contend that intemperance is the cause of every evil which the more favored classes of society may feel or fear. Should this terrible scourge cease its inflictions, at once and universally, I have no belief that the earth would be forthwith Arcadianized, or that the millennium would no longer delay its coming; but still I do believe that the depths of the misery of this vice are yet as far from ever having been fathomed as the deepest parts of the ocean; and that those who have pondered upon it longest and most profoundly have only, as it were, explored a few leagues along the wreck-covered coast of a mighty continent of evil.

Although addressing myself, on this occasion, to men who enjoy both the means and opportunities of understanding and appreciating the highest truths, yet I do not propose to appeal, to any great extent, to those eternal and unchangeable principles which lie under the whole length of existence. Such topics, oppressively weighty, I leave to another profession, or at least to other occasions, — happy if I can now bring a few considerations of a social, political, and economical nature to bear upon the cause of temperance, and can enforce its importance by some of the merest commonplaces of morality.

The man who possesses property presents a broader mark to be struck by the shafts of misfortune or malice. The ears of the poor man are not quick to hear the midnight alarm bell; for he has no warehouses or manufactories in danger of conflagration; and with whatever fury storms may rage along the shore, he has no dread that they will sink any argosies of his. But whenever a man adds new territory to his possessions, he forthwith sends out a colony of hopes and fears to people it. It is as true of any augmentation of wealth as it is of the natural growth of the human body; however much we may increase in size and stature, the living nerves go out to the surface. As an old man dotes upon a child born to him in his decrepitude, so a rich man dotes upon his latest acquisitions of property.

It is obvious that every rich man has the same kind of interest in the future condition of the community, which a merchant has in the freedom from pirates of those seas through which his treasure-laden vessels are sailing. So the value of princely mansions and of insurance stocks must depend somewhat upon the number and pyrotechnic skill of the incendiaries who hold their night-watches in the city. The opulent father leaves, not a blessing, but a curse, to his offspring, if their great patrimony only makes them more obnoxious to general envy, and sharpens a common appetite for plunder, of which they are the objects. Even the blessings of education are but an imperfect boon, if children are to grow up in a community where knowledge is scoffed at, and refinement only provokes insult and libel. What heavier doom could strike a parent's heart than to know that, as soon as he draws his last breath, his children will be banished from their native land, and forced to dwell in some foreign community of lawlessness and profligacy; and yet what is the value of the choice, whether that community shall be abroad, in some foreign realm, *or at home, in the next generation?* Amid corruption of sentiment, and depravity of morals and of manners, a virtuous man is an exile though he remains at home. Surely it is not only one of the highest social duties, but it must be one of the strongest impulses of an intelligent parental affection, to provide a state of society for children, in which, if they prove to be honorable men, they may be honored; and if they prove to be benefactors of their race, they may be revered while living, and mourned when dead. The condition of society which men bequeath to their children gives value or takes it away from all their other bequests.

Look at the relation in which men of eminent talents and genius stand to the present and the coming generations; and see how deep is their interest in the general enlightenment and rectitude of the people. Who are to be their judges and rewarders in a community where all things are decided by the popular voice? Is it not most desirable for such men to live amongst people who measure merit by a scale of truth; who can discern, and will reverence, moral intrepidity and self-sacrifice; who honor mental rather than animal endowments; and who can and will make their best men their first men? Is it nothing for the orator at the capitol, or the author in his closet, to know that he needs not to circumscribe his powers in order to be intelligible to his hearers; but that he addresses a nation for an audience, whose millions of hearts are so many censers, standing always ready to be lighted by the hallowed flame of eloquence? Is it nothing for the poet or the artist to know that the more exquisite and perfect is his work, the more, and not the less, myriads of voices will be added to his fame? Now, all these natural and laudable desires are defeated, to an immense extent, by the wide-spread vice of intemperance. With the rapid decay of all talent, and the extinction of virtuous emotions, in themselves, intemperate men lose the power of appreciating intellectual and moral greatness in others. Their spiritual nature becomes sensualized. Their appetite scourges away every exalted sentiment. Whoever will provide means to slake their thirst; whoever will pervert reason to vindicate their indulgence; whoever will beat down their sincerest well-wishers with the most truculent rage, will be their chosen leaders.

Let intemperate men witness a discussion in the forum or the senate, and you will always see them captivated by the dross of thought, rather than by those golden treasures of wisdom which meditation coins from experience and knowledge. In books, they will generally prefer the obscene blasphemies of Paine to the serene and pious philosophy of Watson. Is it such a tribunal as this which men of talent and genius wish to install or perpetuate?

In all the great questions pertaining to social reform, do not intemperate men almost invariably espouse the side of demoralization? In all efforts for the adornment of society, for the advancement of art, literature, or science, they are antagonist forces. They gravitate towards barbarism. Should they ever obtain a numerical ascendency in any part of our country, they would demolish the temples of science and religion, and banish the priests that minister at their altars. Even now, every intelligent man knows that if the wealth squandered upon this enormous vice were appropriated to the purchase of social libraries, to the founding of mechanics' institutes and supplying them with philosophical apparatus, and to establishing cabinets of the arts and of natural history; and if the time,—that element of priceless value, now a thousand times worse than lost in the haunts of dissipation,—could be devoted to reading well-selected books, to improving conversation, to lyceum exercises, to music and other refining arts, it would, in ten years, give to this republic a new social and political sensorium.

Men of mechanical science and skill are delighted with all new inventions in the useful arts, and are admirers of all new discoveries or applications of philosophical principles. The slightest improvements, — greater simplicity in the construction of a machine, or diminished friction in the revolutions of a wheel, — are sought after with avidity, printed in journals, circulated through the civilized world, and, every where, there is an immediate desire to reduce the improvements to practice. We honor those men whose inventive talents have given, as it were, new organs to mankind, — powers of locomotion by which we travel a hundred times faster and farther than we can with our natural limbs, and a telescopic eye, by which we see objects a million times more remote than with the natural vision. Why do we feel emotions of pride and exultation as we gaze upon those Titan laborers in the service of man, which cleave their "arrowy way" through the sea, from port to port; or, upon the land, take up the burden of ten thousand men, and speed with it, from horizon to horizon, like the horses of the sun? Is it not because they have the power of subserving human interests, of contributing to human amelioration, and of adding, as it were, new capacities to the natural endowments of the race? As a mere matter of taste, how can an intellectual man feel regret at the accidental destruction of an ingenious toy, but experience no sadness at the ruin of the noble faculties of the human mind? How can the merest utilitarian look with sorrow upon the devastations occasioned by an earthquake or a tornado, but regard with indifference the prostration of the lofty capacities of a soul? The spirit of man has been formed in exact correspondence to all the beauty and sublimity of the external world; it has been attuned with divinest skill to all the sacred symphonies of domestic life; it has been made capacious of virtue and happiness. How, on the lowest principles of economical policy, can we see all these divine arrangements baffled, this utility and beauty marred and lost, these heavenly purposes thwarted, without rushing to the rescue, and engaging, if need be, in a lifelong struggle to avert so deplorable a catastrophe?

Behold the lover of the histrionic art, — whose

mind has been stored by careful study and contemplation, with all the archetypes of dramatic excellence. He sees, on the stage, a type of life, a miniature of the world; and night after night he repairs thither, to witness, perhaps for the hundredth time, a representation of the same scenes, — amply rewarded if he can discover some new beauty in gesture, emphasis, or reading. Here he sets up, in his own mind, a standard of perfection, and demands conformity. Nay, his refined taste is pained at aught that is unartistic in plan or execution. The miscasting of a part, by which genius is degraded from its sphere; the suppression of a kindling thought; an emotion lost in a hasty cadence; or even the inelegant elision of a letter, wounds his desire for perfection. As a mere matter of consistency in his own character, and without any reference to duty or principle, how can such a man witness, with indifference, this disorganized, and I might almost say, this intoxicated and besotted drama of human life, as he sees it daily enacted; — the orderly progression of its parts deranged, its pathos made ridiculous and its mirth mournful, its noblest heroes sinking to clowns and fools, and its catastrophes such as nature abhors! One master vice has invaded the scene, and spread disorder through all its parts; and where that vice controls, no noble passages are spoken, no holy sentiments are breathed, no sweet melodies are sung; but chaos reigns, and the brightest stars are stricken down and quenched forever, midway of their glorious course!

When men of education and taste, generalizing their ideas of propriety and beauty, and applying the same rules of judging and of acting to the supreme, that they now apply to the subordinate affairs of men; when they shall look upon the well-ordering of society as they now look upon an improved machine or a well-executed work of art, or even upon a skilful, scenic exhibition of what never existed, then will all the means by which intemperance is diffused or countenanced become the disgust and scorn of mankind. The spreader of pestilential diseases will be esteemed a more tolerable member of the community than the manufacturer or vender of alcoholic drinks.

Addressing myself particularly, on this occasion, to men of intelligence, I may pass unnoticed such facts and considerations as are now familiar to every person of common information. I may therefore abstain from dwelling upon such truths as that three fourths of all the crimes with which society is tormented are caused by intemperance; that we are indebted to the same inexhaustible source of evil for three fourths of all the paupers whose harsh demands have wearied and sickened the spirit of public charity; and that three fourths at least of all those cases of imprisonment for small debts, which, but a few years ago, were so common, and whose aggregate of time would amount to more years than the world has existed, either originated in debts for ardent spirits, or in debts which would have been readily paid but for the disabilities and poverty resulting from their use.

All these, however, and many similar considerations, I shall here omit. Yet what a case it must be, which allows its advocate to forego arguments of such weight and conclusiveness as these! Nor shall I stop to compute the number of persons whom intemperance has incited to dreadful crimes, or bereft of reason, or from whose souls it has, as it were, carved out and cast away all noble qualities, and filled up the vacant spaces with satanic instincts. The squalid throngs whom it daily sends to the receptacles of poverty and revolting wretchedness; the felons, formed of sterner elements, who by violence and midnight depredation earn their sad years of solitude and bondage; the tormented maniacs who rave and howl in their gloomy cells; and the malefactors who crown a life of guilt with a death of ignominy; — these are only a few choice cases, — finished or pattern specimens, — upon whom intemperance has done its perfect work. These are the swiftest runners in the race, who have reached the goal and received the prize. All these victims, with the wretches whom we encounter in our daily intercourse with the world, whom intemperance has clothed with its vassal livery, and taught to gibber in its un-human language, whose flesh it has gangrened to the bone, and whose souls it has corrupted to the core, — all these are but a part, and the smallest part, of the sacrifices offered by society upon the altars of this vice. And yet, in what pagan nation was Moloch ever propitiated by such an unbroken and swift-moving procession of victims, as are offered to this Moloch of Christendom.

It is by the diffusive action of intemperance that I propose to show how society suffers through its whole frame and organization; how the poison of this vice flows through all its circulation, and destroys vitality and joy in all its organs. Intemperance squanders an enormous portion of the resources of the country. The capital spent in the preliminary operations of producing the materials and of manufacturing, purchasing, and vending intoxicating drinks has exceeded the whole civil list expenditures of all our governments, state and national. After having cost so much for production and distribution, its consumption generates a class of persons whose support and punishment equal the amount of the primary outlay. And the value of productive labor annihilated, and the aggregate of losses occasioned, by this consumption, subtract from the available resources of the community a third sum, probably not inferior in magnitude to each of the others. The arm of national industry in agriculture, manufactures, and the mechanic arts, strong and effective as it now is, has neither the powerful enginery of means, nor the mental or muscular vigor to direct and to wield them, which it would otherwise possess. Suppose Robert Fulton had been a sot. Suppose the long, laborious, and secluded period spent by Eli Whitney, in inventing and perfecting the cotton-gin, had been spent in a tap-room! Yet who can doubt that intemperance has robbed our country of many Fultons and many Whitneys? We know that the brightest minds are most subject to its diabolical seducements. Who, in the circle of his own acquaintance, does not remember some shining intellect, some bright orb of mind, rising in splendor, and rapidly ascending to a refulgent day, but suddenly shrouded in everlasting night? Our country owes its incomparable prosperity vastly more to the development of its mental than its physical resources. Indeed, the development of mental power is a prerequisite to the development of physical power. Our territory has limits; improvement through increased intelligence is illimitable. The fertility of the earth is great, but the fertility of the hnman mind is a thousand times greater. Compared with the riches of the latter, the exuberance of the globe is barrenness. Our advancement in the arts and comforts of life springs not from material resources nor from numbers, — not from luxuriant valleys and exhaustless mines, and a redoubling population, — so much as from mental activity, from a general arousing of the intellect of our people. It is the application of intelligence to the mighty agencies of nature, and the enterprise and thrift with which proceeds, when obtained, are reinvested as capital, and thus their reproductive or accumulating powers brought into use; — it is by these means, and such as these, that our country is carried forward in its magnificent career of improvement. But alas! how many thousand sources which would otherwise have contributed to swell the stream of prosperity has intemperance dried up!

This vice has shed a Gothic influence on manners and learning. The universal practice, which heretofore existed, of considering ardent spirits, or some other kind of intoxicating liquors, as a luxury, and relying on their stimulus for excitement on all holidays and at all festive meetings, not only impaired the culture of all such arts and associations as cherish elegance and propriety in manners, and benevolence in sentiment, but it generated positive vulgarity in the intercourse between men, inflamed all combative and riotous propensities, taught a corrupting licentiousness of speech, and granted a monopoly to debasing topics of conversation. Throughout the land, wherever a young man has had a leisure evening or hour, the tempting fiend has whispered in his ear the seductions of the dram-shop. Often has this been his resort, instead of being at home, reading some instructive book with mother and sisters, or in a friend's house with such companions as are striving to obtain more knowledge, and to behave more worthily. And what a large portion of the public mind, as it now exists, has been filtrated through these anti-clarifiers, these anti-refiners, where all its gentleness, its modesty, and purity, have been strained off and sluiced away, and only a corrosive, polluted, mephitic sediment preserved! Nor has it fared better with the cause of learning, than with elegance of manners or refinement of feeling. No ray of it can ever penetrate the opaque soul of intemperance. The *desire* of knowledge is the magnet that attracts it. Wherever this desire is craving, it will attract knowledge into the mind through every obstruction, and even though the natural inlets of the senses are closed against it. It seems to be a law of nature, that wherever this desire of knowledge can be excited, it is no longer possible so to insulate the human soul as to prevent its access. It will find a conductor; or, if it can find no conductor, it will, like the condensed electricity of a thunder cloud, leap a vacuum to reach the object that attracts it. But intemperance extirpates this desire. Under its influence, the love of knowledge not only ceases, but deceases; or, what is worse, its nature is so transformed that it seeks only bitter or pernicious knowledge.

Another idea seems not irrelevant to this topic. Both men and children acquire with great facility and rapidity until they rise about to the common level. There the mass stops. Only minds of uncommon energy rise higher, and those with difficulty. But transfer a common mind to a society where the general standard is higher than itself, and it will forthwith rise to the common level again; and then it will again cease its ascent. Whatever, then, depresses the common standard of attainment or intelligence, weighs down all that is above, depresses all that is below, and causes an aggregate of loss which is incalculable. Not only has general intelligence been circumscribed, and general refinement debased, but the whole circle of social, every-day virtues, — order, forbearance, sympathy, charitableness, conscientiousness, — have lost tone, wakefulness, and decision. In myriads of hearts, the same cause has baffled all the benign influences of Christianity. It is not extravagant to say that civilization, in this country, is now a century behind what it would have been, if ardent spirits had never been known amongst us. I do not mean that species of civilization whose only evidences consist in a few prodigies of learning, or a few great masters in the elegant arts, with a small metropolitan circle of courtly gentlemen, while all around is passion, and ignorance, and superstition. All this, where this is all, is but mockery. But I mean the civilization which consists in a love of order and of duty, and in that recognition and sacred regard for the rights of others which cannot be enforced by law; in affectionate hearts, in active, truth-loving minds, — all combining to make happy families, brotherly neighborhoods, and a great and incorruptible people. This kind of civilization has already been postponed a century, in our land, by the barbarizing effects of intemperance.

Let me ask men whose reason has been developed and strengthened by education, for what end that reason was given them. Is it not one main office and function of reason to mark the relation between Causes and Effects? Do not talented and educated men value themselves, and does not the community, with one consent, yield them deference and respect, because of their sagacity and foresight in predicting the future from a knowledge of the present? Effects sometimes follow causes instantaneously; sometimes effects are separated from their causes by long intervals of time, or wide regions of space. But, to the eye of reason, these intervening periods or spaces, however vast they may be, are nothing. Reason recognizes the effect as linked to the cause, and as happening in immediate succession to it, though separated by the distance of centuries, or by the circumference of the globe. It matters not whether I fire a magazine by a slow match or a quick one; the moment the explosion takes place, I cannot deny that I caused it. Enlightened reason cannot help apprehending the truth in an instant, that whoever is responsible for the origin is responsible for the result; and that a man who occupies a period of five or of ten years in turning his neighbor into a devil, is as really guilty of effecting the diabolical transformation of that neighbor, as though he had put the horns and hoofs upon him at one operation.

In the present state of our experience on this subject, every intelligent man foreknows the fatal consequences of importing, manufacturing, selling, and drinking ardent spirits, with as much certainty as an astronomer foreknows an eclipse. When I was a practitioner at the bar, I well recollect that, in three counties of Massachusetts, during a period of about six months, three murders were committed, and two men, one of them having a wife and children, were executed for the crime of arson. In each case, the perpetrator was in a state of intoxication; and, humanly speaking, not one of these crimes would have been perpetrated, but for the intoxication. But the terrors of these few, though awful crimes, do not bear comparison with the nameless and innumerable sufferings and wrongs which, during the same period, were inflicted upon the innocent members of society by the same cause.

And by what means do all this guilt and woe come upon mankind? The answer is plain. Some wealthy merchants import liquor from abroad, that they may increase their wealth. Some capitalists, from the nutritious grains, and the cooling fruits of the earth, distil it at home, that they may add to their capital. The legislature invests certain subordinate tribunals with discretionary power to grant so many licenses, "as the public good," — yes, *as the public good*, for such is the blasphemous phraseology of the law, — may require. Some owners of real estate, opulent and educated men, because they can obtain higher rents, and many men, because such has long been their occupation, importune the municipal and county authorities to grant licenses, *for one year only*. To men who are themselves comfortably and happily situated, one year is not long, and the licenses are granted. Forthwith, every licensed person repairs to his appointed place, opens the fountains of destruction, and the work begins. In one region, a peaceful citizen is butchered; in another, midnight blazes with conflagration; in a third, the earthquake voice of riot is heard, at its work of demolition; — from all sides, a rushing sound of affright and contention afflicts the ear, mingled with such groans of agony as never came from the dark temples of the Druids, where human victims were sacrificed by hundreds. This process seems simple. And, my friends, it is simple, yea, horrible in its simplicity. And it is as fatal as it is simple. The death-warrant that goes out from the executive chamber, under the sign-manual of the governor, and authenticated by the great seal of the state, commanding the sheriff to do execution upon the body of a malefactor, is not more certain to be executed upon that body, than, under our present laws and usages, these evils are to be inflicted, with each returning season, upon the body of society.

At that annual meeting of our city and county officers, at which, according to law and custom, licenses are generally granted, after the last petitioner has received his charter of destruction, and retired, and while the official dignitaries who have granted it are left for a moment alone, suppose their reason should faithfully perform its office, by bringing causes and effects together; — by presenting, in the very room where the licenses had been granted, the effect of those licenses for the coming year. Suppose that, on closing the book where their decisions are recorded, suddenly, quick as thought, a terrific vision of the future consequences of their conduct should start into living reality before them. Here, a murderer darts athwart the room, and hews down his victim before their eyes. There, the outbursting flame reveals the flying incendiary. Here, caged beneath their feet, howl and shriek the victims of delirium. On this side of the tribunal, the gray hairs of a parent are brought down with sorrow to the grave, by the worse than parricidal blows of an impious son. On that side welters in his own blood the desperate suicide. Apart and alone, her frame convulsed with unspeakable agonies, and her tearful eyes covered with her hands, kneels, and prays with unavailing prayer, the once happy wife. Song and smile no longer come unbidden to her lips. She seeks seclusion; she flies from sympathy; for the voice of the tenderest consolation tortures her like fire. Where now are those burning vows of love, those attestations of undying fidelity, which imprecated the vengeance of

Heaven on their violation?—vows and attestations which she had garnered in her heart's heart, and made an idol-treasure. These priceless pearls, they too have been stolen and melted in the cup of abomination. See, all around, those groups of desolate children! Hunger and nakedness have been their father's love, and snow and winter's storms their mother's breast and song. But I will not, I cannot delineate these intolerable realities. They cannot be spoken by mortal tongue; they cannot be conceived by mortal mind; no, though all that poets and divines have said of the place of final retribution were concentrated in one focal thought;—for neither in the Christian's nor in the pagan's hell are the innocent made chief sufferers!

Were intemperance stripped of every evil attribute, save its cruelty to children alone, how could it then be tolerated, even for a day, by any truly Christian people? The condition of the children of intemperate parents seems, of itself, an argument of sufficient power to revolutionize a world. Maternal nature has filled the hearts of children full of happy promises. A presentiment of love is a divine instinct in their bosoms. They are created expectant of joy, awaiting it as the new-strung Æolian awaits the zephyr. Nature enjoins no obligation upon us with a more earnest and articulate voice than when she commands and implores us through the helplessness and trustingness of infancy and childhood. Who needs an interpreter, to read in their feebleness the duty of protection? Does not a child's proneness to imitate whatever it witnesses, and to believe whatever it is taught, admonish us, that it should witness nothing unworthy of imitation, nor be taught from the volumes of selfishness and depravity? And when a sunny look so fills the heart of a child with joy, that it overflows through the face and agitates the whole frame, is it no revelation to us, that gentleness should be its atmosphere, and smiles and caresses the ambrosial food of its spirit? Why, then, when children first awaken to a consciousness of being, should they be seized in the iron arms of pain! Why, even in the dwelling of a parent, should their sweet affections be without a home! Why brand and burn in upon the opening tablets of their minds the characters of anger, and malevolence, and impiety? What wild rebellion against every impulse of natural affection, against every law of God, to suffer that monster-parent, the drunkard, to pour out upon the tender fibres of their hearts his bitter and scalding wrath; to subject their fragile and trembling frames to his explosive passions, and to the redoubled blows of his iron hand! The every-day scenes enacted in the home of a drunkard teach children, as far as they can be taught, to think wrongly, to feel wrongly, and to act wrongly; and what else do we need to complete our idea of a fiend? This is indeed sacrilege; for it is a desecration of the temple of the spirit. Why do our unequal statutes punish infanticide, and yet tolerate the infliction of this moral death? How long before the laws of nature will cease to be suspended; how long must the air remain a non-conductor of sound; how long must light cease to be reflected from suffering infancy and childhood, so that we can hear their pleadings and behold their sorrows, as they exhibit their wretchedness and pour out their supplications, by the side of our daily walks! To what higher wrong could the Savior have referred when he said, rather than that a man should offend one of these little ones, it were better that a millstone were hanged about his neck, and that he were cast into the depths of the sea!

It is the opinion of many intelligent men that the present times are full of evil auguries.

Violence, to a fearful extent, has usurped the place of law. Many alarming cases have occurred, where fraud and perjury have invaded the civil franchise, and suborned the ballot-box to utter lying responses. The land-pirates whom we call "*lynchers*" are multiplying. That hideous thing, a mob, more terrible than any fabled monster of the ancients, has suddenly appeared, in almost every city in the land, committed its ravages, and then vanished, to reäppear for its work of havoc, we know not where or when. These are evil portents. In one respect, these harbingers of ill are most unwelcome and ominous; for if they are not, in themselves, greater enormities than ever happened before, they have certainly followed each other, within a few years past, with unprecedented frequency. But I confess, I see nothing in them all, which, if other things must remain as they are, ought not so to be. I could have no faith in the production of good results by good means, if bad means did not produce bad results. Whoever wishes consequences to be changed, without a corresponding change in antecedents, wishes a violation of the laws of nature. There are but two methods of curbing or subduing the unlawful propensities of men; either by an external or by an internal power; either by the law of force or by the law of duty. In most of the countries of Europe, the rulers adopt the surgical system; and, *for that system*, they use the appropriate instruments, — the horse-guards, the *gendarmerie*, and the Siberian mines. Here we profess to adopt the preventive system. Universal education is our theoretical substitute for standing armies. Instead of policemen, traversing every road and street, we propose the early inculcation of virtuous principles upon the minds of the young. Schoolhouses are the republican line of fortifications. And yet, in flagrant violation of all these pretensions and assumptions, we legalize and uphold a system, in relation to intoxicating drinks, which counterworks the influence of all virtuous education, engenders a spirit of universal lawlessness, and multiplies, a thousand fold, the potency of all dissocial passions. We seem to forget, that in a government like ours, it is, primarily, the condition of the public mind that constitutes our weal or woe. We forget that no external lawlessness or anarchy can ever exist, without being heralded by lawlessness and anarchy in the passions of the people. The external is only an embodiment or *actualizing* of the precedent internal. And yet, while we continue to apply a stimulus by which the fever is aggravated to delirium, we tremble at the consequences of the insanity we are ourselves creating. Let there be an entire abstinence from intoxicating drinks throughout this country during the period of a single generation, and a mob would be as impossible as combustion without oxygen. In our now dishonored cities, history alone would inform posterity, that, morally speaking, they were dwelling within the crater of extinct volcanoes.

There are fixed and immutable principles which are applicable to the conduct of society, not less than to that of individuals. These principles the whole collected force of mankind can neither annul nor suspend. We might as well attempt to change the rising or the setting of the sun by the major vote of the people. Society, indeed, has an option whether to place itself within the action of one class of principles or of another; but, once having chosen its position, the wheel of destiny rolls on, and bears it forward with inexorable force. If a community will make wise provision for that vast influx of spiritual nature which flows in with the birth of its children, and which is becoming a part of its administrative authority, just as fast as those children emerge from pupilage and assume the prerogatives of manhood; then these silent forces of nature, — by a law as certain as that which sustains the ever-moving spheres, — will bear it upward along a glorious, ascending scale of grandeur and felicity. But if society chooses to neglect the minds of children, and to infuriate the passions of men, its years of tribulation and anguish are predestined by an adamantine law of necessity. Our government could not survive for a single year with such a population as exists in Italy or Ireland. We have no artificial, graduated distinctions, among the members of our community, assigning higher platforms to higher classes, where the one above is not only surrounded by bulwarks of its own, but is placed, as it were, beyond striking distance from the one below.

Our citizens, whether they regard substance or not, are all educated to despise forms. All our political and most of our social institutions amplify and stimulate the feeling of self-importance in the individual, — a feeling of elevating power, if properly balanced and controlled; but, if unchastened and inflamed, the very instrument of aggression and lawlessness. Amidst the general ignorance of Europe, the notions about human rights cannot be so wrong as they may be with us; for false conclusions which have been arrived at through the forms of reasoning are infinitely worse than blind impulses. The former have the force of all the propensities, sanctioned by the intellect. The uneducated millions of Europe are nothing to the politician. Here they vote, and are, therefore, the real Warwicks, or king-makers. There, they are beneath the attention of the demagogues who flatter and inflame. Here, there is a competition among miscreants to flatter and inflame, in order that they may lead. There, the flagitious are separate atoms, without cohesion or sympathy. Here, through our political organization, though scattered over the whole Union, they can concentrate their entire force into one blow, and direct it to any point. There, they suffer under the common paralysis of despotism. Here, they are imbued with the vigor of our free institutions, and are effervescent with the vitality of an intense life. There, they are unarmed, and are outside of the citadel of government. Here, they are armed; they are within the citadel; they help to name the sentinels; they have access to the torch and the magazine. If the more favored classes of our society will do nothing to arrest the progress of intemperance, which, more than all things else, creates bad men, and makes bad men worse, they may well tremble for the institutions of their country, for their property, and for their families. They occupy no such high table-land of security, that the billows of popular commotion will break below their feet. The tumults, the outbreaks of violence, which have already happened, are only tremulous vibrations, foretokening the earthquake that is yet to come. Fiercer paroxysms will ensue;—such shocks from beneath as will upheave the foundations of law and order, unseat the tribunals of justice, and dash the hostile masses of society against each other, as though the steady earth itself were unbalanced, and were rocking and plunging in its orbit.

The past experience of mankind has not left us without some fundamental axioms in social economy. If there be any fidelity in the laws of nature, we may rest assured that the mass of citizens who possess comfort and competence,—the yeoman with his unencumbered and well-stocked farm; the mechanic with his profitable trade and his complement of tools; and also all those engaged in mercantile pursuits, who can truly speak of their own shop and their own goods,—will never knowingly conspire to subvert the very laws on which their right to their own property reposes. So, too, all young men, who commence life without property, but who are conscious of the habits of industry, honesty, and temperance, which will most certainly result in the acquisition of property, will never offer themselves as recruits at any agrarian camp. Neither will any intelligent and upright citizen ever claim an equal share, by his vote, in regulating the machinery of government, together with a reserved right, that if, at any time, this machine does not move to suit his fancy, he may violently wrest it from its course, or dash it in pieces. We know, too, that there can be no such security upon earth as sober-minded, staid citizens, capable of impartial thought, strenuous for the right, and feeling that the maintenance of public order and justice is the only guaranty for the well-being of themselves and of their children. On the other hand, too, we know that the slaves of a selfish appetite, who have spent all their own property in criminal indulgences, occupy the same relation towards the prosperity of others, as, in the animal kingdom, the vulture occupies towards the dove. Their *beau ideal* of a republic is to divide all property equally, and when they have spent their share, *to divide again.*

But perhaps the more favored classes of

society will say, We deplore the evil that surrounds us, but we are not responsible for its existence; our advantageous position secures us from the poverty and the wretchedness you delineate, and we can maintain, within our own charmed circle, the institutions and the usages which will secure enjoyment and dignified ease amongst ourselves, as well as deference from without; and, should the hordes of intemperance ever invade our sphere, we can trust to our united power and to a sense of common danger to repel them. But let these classes scan their position more narrowly, and see if, in truth, there is any barrier, any border-waste, or sanitary cordon, between them and those natural enemies to their welfare, whom intemperance engenders. Some of the malefactors of past years, we know, have expiated their crimes by an ignominious death, and others are now making penal atonement in the solitude of jails and prisons; but where now are the malefactors of coming years? Where now are the murderers, the incendiaries, the felonious burglars or assaulters, — the wretched victims of intemperance in all their hideous variety, who are to make the year that begins to-day like the years that are past? They walk the streets by your side; they follow, at your heels, into the crowd; they are now making themselves acquainted with your property and its places of deposit, the better to mature their schemes of plunder; they obtain their implements of mischief at the shops rented by yourselves; they drink in the depravity, prolific of all their deeds, at places which you have opened for its sale; and before to-morrow's sun shall set, somebody will feel the blow, which they will strike, in his property, or, it may be, in his heart.

But outrage and violence are not invariable concomitants of this enemy of mankind. Suppose jurors or witnesses become corrupt, or vehemently prejudiced, because you are rich and they are poor, or because you are learned and they are ignorant; you may be plundered through the forms of law as certainly as by a body of Turkish Janizaries. Who can feel secure, when his property, his life, or his reputation depends upon a witness from whose mind intemperance has eradicated all moral principle, as colors are extracted by chemical agents? If a fact decisive of an important cause is known to an intemperate witness, it can be washed out of his mind by a quart of rum; and if such a fact be wanted by a fraudful litigant, rum will give to such a witness an extemporaneous memory. Those conversant with courts well know that large amounts of property have often been lost, and enduring stigmas have been fixed upon pure characters, by testimony wholly alcoholic in its origin. Often, too, has the assertion of valuable rights been foregone, because intemperance had besotted the witness by whose testimony alone they could have been established. In commercial affairs, what vast amounts of property frequently depend upon the evidence of men whose powers of clear recollection and of precise and intelligent statement are wholly obliterated, though something of the moral sense may have survived, or have been renovated in them! We all feel that a reputation for honor, and virtue, and beneficent action is the third treasure in the universe, inferior only to the smiles of Heaven and the approbation of conscience; and yet, when the profligate in principle or the dissolute in life are found contending with the sober and the upright, do not the intemperate almost invariably espouse the cause of the former? In some parts of our country, numerous instances have already occurred where that sympathy with guilt, which is generated by intemperance more than by all other things combined, has filled the temples of justice with a rout of fraternal villains, rebelling against law, perplexing the minds of witnesses with fear, and overawing the sworn administrators of justice. Nor is it unworthy of remark, in this connection, that the established and regularly-organized tribunals of the land have jurisdiction of only a small part of the controversies which arise among men. The law takes no cognizance of innumerable questions which relate to the performance of domestic, social, or neighborhood duties. In these cases, all persons are arraigned and tried, literally by the *vicinage*. Moral character, the peace of individuals for life, the quiet of families, the fate of happy friendships, are often involved in these extrajudicial adjudications from which there is no appeal. And what is the part which the intemperate enact in these local controversies? Are they not pretty surely to be found speaking with lying tongues, maligning all men who oppose the system which feeds their appetites, placarding their assassin handbills at the corners of the streets, and profaning the sacred reputation of mothers and daughters?

In treating so solemn a subject as this, I utterly disclaim even the remotest allusion to partisan politics or partisan leaders; and yet I may be permitted to appeal to the observation of every honest man of all parties, whether, in our general or local elections, — those for governor and legislators, or those for county and municipal offices, — in cases, too, where success or defeat will stand as the verdict of the public, convicting or acquitting of some great moral or political delinquency, the intemperate man will not always vote for the candidate who will bribe him with a glass of rum, or who will promise to use his influence in favor of the system which will give him a glass of rum, rather than for his sober competitor, who advocates the cause of temperance as the only foundation of law and order. So, too, if there be a newspaper, which advocates all crimes by advocating an increase of the cause of all crimes, which scoffs at religion in the pulpit, libels justice on the bench, and merges the moral welfare of the state in the success of a party, or the triumph of its candidate at an election, that newspaper is sure to be the intemperate man's oracle. And it is only because the intemperate are so numerous and powerful as a party, that here and there a sober miscreant places himself at their head, and defends them and their cause, because such an employment is a safer, though not a less ignominious method of obtaining his daily bread, than highway robbery or passing counterfeit money.

It can never be sufficiently impressed upon those who are prone to feel that they have no direct interest in the general condition of the community, that when they have seen all poorhouses, all jails and prisons, and the gallows itself, they have not yet seen a hundredth part of the diffusive evils of intemperance. These outward and visible evidences of crime are but topical inflammations, cutaneous eruptions, exhibiting themselves on the surface of the body politic only after a mortification, which began at the vitals, has reached the circumference. In the social state, not even the purest virtue can secure happiness, or an immunity from danger, to any one class, while vice abounds in another. There are nerves which extend through the whole body politic, and when any member is wounded, the pain will circuit the whole body politic. The favored classes may think they occupy favored apartments in the ship; but, if it does founder, the state-room will go down with the steerage. Every man, though living in his own dwelling, with his fee-simple deeds under Hobbs's lock and key, is a mere tenant at will of the incendiary. It is of the very nature of malice, and envy, and revenge, that they claim to be rightful owners of all property and character, and to destroy either at their own good pleasure. How can any merchant feel secure, in committing his deep-freighted vessels to the sea, if intemperance is to preside at the helm or command from the quarter deck? Is not the ocean already inlaid with treasures, — ay, and with human sacrifices too, — which intemperance, more remorseless than tempests and hidden rocks, has sent down to its unapproachable garners?

Nor let the wealthy and the talented flatter themselves that they can purchase any amulet whose potent charm shall save their own households from the common destroyer. Should they escape themselves, have they made any covenant with the demon that he will spare their children? A rich inheritance will only make the means of destruction so much the more accessible. The wealth which the merchant or the professional man is toiling to amass, in order that he may bequeath it, may only buy the sparkling wine in which his children will dissolve the pearl of reputation, or may only purchase the golden goblet from which they will drain perdition. In the whole circle of human calamities, what more mournful spectacle are we compelled to behold, than to see the sons of opulence, just as they are emerging into manhood, when their hearts should glow and burn to run the race of usefulness and honor; — what spectacle, I ask, is more mournful, than to see them, as we sometimes do, torn from a father's care and from a mother's love, and actually exiled from home and country, that they may be subjected to the stern discipline of a whale ship, or a man-of-war, because they cannot walk unharmed amid the burning ploughshares with which we have tessellated the soil of the pilgrims? Nor even in exile are they safe. Some have perished vilely in a drunken brawl upon a foreign shore, and strangers' hands have dug their unhallowed grave. The lofty and indomitable spirit of others has dashed them to death against the bars of their iron cage. Some return, but with extinguished faculties, now alike incapable of good or ill. Human guilt has carbonized the diamond, but from the ashes no human skill can rekindle its pristine fires. But, as sometimes happily has been true, should the wanderer, after years of absence and harsh discipline, return, to cause the sun, as it sets after a life of storm, to shine brightly upon his father's house, — is it nothing that, for years, a whole family have nightly laid their heads upon a pillow of thorns, and that daily their hearts have yearned as they beheld the vacant seat at the table and at the fireside? Is it nothing that *he*, for years, has been a wanderer from the paths of rectitude? And though a reäscension to virtue may gain the forgiveness of men and of God, yet is it nothing that, in his own memory,—that Book of Judgment for us all,—the indelible record of his sins will remain forever? Blame not these youthful victims of our cruel institutions. The sin is ours. I repeat it, *the sin is ours*. It is we who dig the pitfalls, amongst which their impetuous and inexperienced feet cannot safely walk. Alas! in what a world do we live, that neither in the land of our nativity, nor any where on the broad surface of the globe, is there any refuge or hiding-place from this all-ingulfing ruin!

Surrounded as the young men of the present day have been by perpetual and domineering temptations to fall into intemperate habits, is it to the uncertain tenure of their honor and fidelity that refined and educated parents can confide the worldly happiness of their daughters, without a fear? Though all earthly auspices smile propitiously upon their happy nuptials, what angel has lifted up the curtain of the future, and assured their eyes that, suddenly, upon the paradise of wedded love there shall not arise the hell of domestic discord? Why do parents gather together all the riches of their own happiness, and treasure them in a beautiful daughter's life; why do they spend uncounted wealth to give her a dowry, gemmed with every personal and moral attraction; why strive to encompass her with a celestial atmosphere of purity and faith; why set an angelic guard of watchfulness and love around her daily steps, and yet remain wholly insensible to *that condition of society* where the deadliest enemies to her future happiness are lying in ambush? No father, no mother, loves son or daughter,—not any man loves any child, *with an intelligent and forecasting love*, who does not feel it to be as important to diminish the temptations of that state of society, into which these children must soon enter, as it is to arm them with moral strength to resist those temptations.

Every man, who prefers any claim to the courtly title of *gentleman*, has an indispensable duty to perform on the subject of temperance. There have been ages of the world when great physical hardihood, and a general predominance in men of the animal nature over the spiritual, made habits of intemperance infinitely less hideous and repulsive, than they are in these days of comparative mental progress and social refinement. Every ray of moral and intellectual light that beams upon society makes the contrast more palpable between the loathsome exhibitions of this vice, and that elegance and dignified simplicity of manners which belong to a truly civilized life. Conduct which was then only a fault is now a disgrace. What then excited but little more than rebuke is now worthy of penal retribution and consuming scorn.

The semi-barbarism, sometimes seen at the present day, whenever it is the effect of hereditary ignorance, rudeness, and poverty, is entitled to an indulgent judgment. I feel a sentiment of pity overmastering that of indignation, when I see the poor and ignorant seeking, through the indulgences of appetite, a transient oblivion of their cares and sorrows. They do not at all comprehend the magnitude of their error. Human nature demands excitement. Of this they are conscious, while they know but imperfectly of any other resource save animal pleasures. But there is no such palliation for the wealthy and the educated. They are relieved from all the ignoble necessities of existence. They have ten thousand captivating resources at command. The lessons of wisdom which blaze forth on every side of the universe summon them to high contemplations and noble deeds, as with the voice of the seraphim. Their just sphere is more and more distant from all low and animal indulgences. Is *that* a *gentleman*, who, but an hour ago, seemed worthy to discuss immortal themes of philosophy with Plato, or Socrates, or Bacon, but whose collapsed frame now falls to the earth, whose mind and heart sink into regions of stupidity, and drivelling folly, and profanity, and all hateful and vile impurities, until the foul spirit of drunkenness, as though, at last, disgusted with its own foul work, hides itself in a mimic death? How hateful and irredeemable such a transformation! And how suddenly and certainly every intemperate man, whatever may have been his education and sphere of life, will discard all rules of propriety and decorum for the indulgence of his appetite! For what is fitness of time, of place, or of occasion; what is cleanliness of person or of garb; what is dignity of manners; what are beauty and adaptation of language, to him who hesitates not to wallow with the swine; and who, out of the noble and godlike faculty of speech, has not preserved so much as the swine's power of articulation? "Drunk," says Shakspeare, "drunk, and speak parrot, and squabble, swagger, swear, and discourse fustian with one's own shadow.— To be now a sensible man, by and by a fool, and presently a beast!" Suppose, at the close of that procession of all living animals which passed in review before Adam to receive their respective names, that a hurdleful of these "drunken gentlemen" had been drawn along; would not the father of our race, smitten with disgust at the objects, and with indignation at the insult, have rushed away and committed suicide, to prevent the possibility of any such monsters ever proceeding from himself?

And is the legislation which tolerates, is that administration of the law which encourages, are those departments of business and those usages of society which inflict this reeking abomination upon mankind,— are these the boasted fruits of six thousand years of experience and of progress? Who dares to teach children, at home or at the Sabbath school, that it is eighteen hundred years since the commencement of the Christian era, when we all know that the Sabbath is the benefit-day of the rum-seller, and the very Saturnalia of drunkenness? Is it from its preëminence in crimes and debaucheries, and in thousand-tongued blasphemy, that the Sabbath is called the *first* day of the week? It almost seems as though it were by way of insult and mockery that, in some of our states, in the very chapter of the statute book, which sustains the whole scheme of rum-selling, the Sabbath is called the Lord's day. Consult the records of the Police Court, ask the officers of justice on Monday morning, and they will tell you whose day the Sabbath has been, in facts that leave no doubt about the patron's name.

And now, my friends, in view of these appalling evils, which make our past history look black, and threaten to blacken our future history also, what is to be done? I speak as a practical and religious man, to practical and religious men; and, in profound anxiety, I ask, What is to be done? We have a right to expect the blessing of God upon all our wise efforts for reform; but we have no right to expect reform through a miracle of God, superseding our own exertions. Governments have essayed to stop the ravages of this enemy, but they have hitherto failed. It is more than two centuries since Massachusetts commenced the method of regulating or licensing the sale of intoxicating drinks. In this she has been followed by the other states; but during all this period, drunkenness, with all its woes, has abounded; and probably its victims at the present time are relatively more numerous than when the first licensing law was enacted. Regulation has not regulated it. Licensing for the "public good" has proved to be licensing for both public and private evil. And besides, this system has given birth to a vast amount of collateral crime. Evasions of public law, always to be deprecated, perjury, tampering with jurors, and corrupting the pure channels of justice, have been its constant and woful retinue. Because, then, its concomitants have been evil, and its results inefficient for good, I hold that, after an experiment of two hundred years, we are admonished, nay, required to adopt some other plan.

Some philanthropists, — among whom was that excellent man, Dr. Woodward, late superintendent of the Worcester Hospital, who wrote a series of essays on the subject for the press, — have proposed the erection of a Hospital for Inebriates, like a hospital for the insane, where the victims of intemperance can be sequestered from the walks of men, until the fire which alcohol has kindled in their bodies can be quenched. While honoring the benevolence of this suggestion, I have never seen reason to adopt it. Why incur vast expenditures for machinery to inject disease into the body politic, and then repeat the expenditure to apply a remedy? Instead of the unnatural process of turning sober men into drunkards, at an immense outlay of human happiness and wealth, and then attempting to turn the drunkards back again into sober men by another outlay, why not keep the sober men sober, in the first instance, and thus save all cost of the machinery, partial losses in all cases, and total loss in many? I would not contract a consumption, even if an experimenter could prescribe a certain, instead of his uncertain nostrums for my cure. I would not melt a purse of gold and mingle it with dross, even on the mint-master's assurance that he would refine it and coin it for circulation again. And for better reasons than these, I would not consent to forfeit years of happiness, and incur loathsome degradation and consuming pain, even though God himself would assure me by one miracle that he would restore me by another.

My friends, the only true and proper Asylum for Inebriates has been constructed. It was constructed in the year 1850, in the state of Maine. Neil Dow was the builder, — a nobler architect than Sir Christopher Wren, or those who poised the dome of St. Peter's in the upper air. It is the grandest Asylum ever erected or conceived; for its base embraces the whole territorial area of the state; its walls are coëxtensive with the boundaries of the state, and it has a dome no less lofty and resplendent than the arch of heaven above. Wherever the means of inebriation are excluded, there is the true asylum for inebriates. Massachusetts and Rhode Island have spread the protecting arches of this roof over their soil. The youthful territory of Minnesota has already done the same, — like a young man resolved to be strong and great, and therefore taking the early vow that promises wisdom and length of days. I trust that the "Excelsior" State of New York is about to follow their example, and to become an Empire State in morals as well as in power; and then, from the ocean to the great lakes, water, and not fire, shall be the nourisher of man, and joy, and not woe, the companion of his household.

The meeting of two conditions is always necessary in the formation of a drunkard, — Appetite and Opportunity. Take away either of these conditions, and a drunkard is impossible. Remove appetite, and a man may dwell his life long, unharmed, amid the flowing and ubiquitous ruin. On the other hand, though the appetite exists, yet if the opportunity for indulging it be taken away, it will soon cease its cravings, and then die out. Now, the old license system took away neither opportunity nor appetite. Not taking away the opportunity, it left the appetite the means of self-perpetuation; not extinguishing the appetite, the opportunity became a certain peril. The hospital system proposed to take only the victims already made, and place them for a time out of the way of opportunity; but, at the end of the curative process, it proposed to place them back within the danger of the opportunity;—into the very mouth of the lion from whose jaws they had been plucked; and what was worse still, it left opportunity and appetite to work their ruin upon the other members of society. The Maine law removes opportunity from all, not only from those who are whole, but from those who are sick, and is, therefore, at once both prevention and cure.

Take another view of the subject: It is not within the powers or functions of government to foresee who will commit murders and arsons, who will destroy the peace of families and of society, who will arouse shrieks of woe and lamentation in hearts of innocence and love, and then, having foreseen who these enemies are, to collect them all into one great Aceldama, or Field of Blood, and there destroy them, for prevention's and for humanity's sake; instead of waiting till their cup of crime is full, and then destroying them through retribution. But it is within the proper powers and functions of government to search out those fatal beverages which stimulate to all crimes and inflict all sufferings, and give them to destruction. If we would not doom the one to the gallows, let us doom the other to the gutter. If we recoil from taking human blood, we can take the blood of the vine before it maddens the human. If we may not dash out a man's brains in order to destroy a passion that lurks in his mind, we may dash in the heads of rum puncheons and brandy casks. It is terrible to inflict capital punishment on a fellow-creature, but mere pastime to inflict it on a gin barrel. The ever-living beauty and excellence of the Maine law is, that it is prevention instead of cure, — that it kills the fiend before he gets into the man, instead of waiting till we have to kill the man in order to expel the fiend.

And further; this law digs up the Upas tree by the roots, while all our previous laws only trimmed off a few of its leaves. Taking the whole history of our country, I cannot doubt that, for every glass for which the illicit trader has been punished, he has sold hogsheads with impunity. The fines on the unsuccessful violations of law have been compensated more than a hundred times over by the profits on the successful. If so, then the force of the temptation has been to that of the restraint as more than a hundred to one; and surely, incitements far less urgent than these are sufficient to tempt bad men to destroy their fellow-men, and to stab society in its vitals. But under the ampler protection of the new law, if one gill be sold by the owner, from a warehouse or a ship load, the whole stock or cargo may be confiscated and destroyed. The importer or vender may refuse to take the pledge of teetotalism himself, but we can administer it to his premises. Ask the agonized Laocoon, — and every father of an intemperate child is a greater sufferer than Laocoon, — what is the difference between killing the serpents after they have strangled his children, and crushing them in the egg!

Objection has been made that the Maine law invades natural rights. It restricts natural powers; but I deny that it invades natural rights. In a state of nature, men have the power to do wrong; but neither in a state of nature, nor in society, can any man have a *right* to do *wrong;* and if the evil consequences of actions are any test of their moral quality, what greater crime or calamity has ever existed amongst us than the unrestrained traffic and use of intoxicating drinks?

It has been further objected to this law that it permits sales for certain purposes, while it prohibits them for other purposes; as though there were any necessary contradiction or inconsistency in this. Those who make this objection must judge of the moral quality of conduct by looking at the outward act, instead of inquiring into its object or motive. Our statute book, the common law, and the divine law abound in precedents, and principles too, which refute so obvious a fallacy. We are surrounded by precedents and principles which allow acts under one set of circumstances, that they prohibit and punish under another set of circumstances. The manufacturer of gunpowder may make it in the country, but he cannot make it in the city; and the dealer in this article may store it in the former place, but not in the latter. I believe all the states have licensed lotteries and the sale of lottery tickets; while, at the same time, they forbid the sale of tickets of unlicensed lotteries; and now, a few states, having awakened to a more adequate sense of their mischiefs, prohibit all lotteries and all sales of lottery tickets whatever. New York has incorporated such a provision into her state constitution. For medical and scientific purposes, the physiologist describes the human form in words, and delineates it in pictures; and his books are found, without offence, on the shelves of the professional man and in public libraries; but if the selfsame plates are put into obscene books, accompanied by such descriptions as may excite impure imaginations or corrupt the mind of youth, they may be lawfully seized and destroyed. The cohabitation of unmarried persons is one of the gravest of moral offences; but the moment the ceremony of marriage is performed, this impure relation is converted into one of the holiest on earth. Here is the same external state of life in both cases; yet the one is hallowed and the other punished, because of their different object and motive. God discriminates in the same way. The fourth commandment in the decalogue says, "Six days shalt thou labor;" but on the seventh, "thou shalt not do any work." Why cannot the objector meet this with the exact logical formula of the liquor dealer's sophistry, and say, — *Work is right, or it is not right; if right, why prohibit it at all; if not right, why command it at all?*

Our justifying analogy is plain and complete. Intoxicating liquors, for certain purposes, mechanical and medicinal, are good, and may be used; but for the human organism, and to be taken as beverages, they concentrate all evil, and are therefore abolished.

I have heard it further alleged that the law is unequal, as between the rich and the poor; because the former can appeal and give bonds, while the latter, not having the pecuniary ability to give bonds, must be committed. But why is such an argument urged against this law, when, if it has aught of validity, it would overthrow every law of the land, of which bail is an incident? In all cases whatever, whether criminal or civil, where bail can be demanded, the rich man can give it, while the poor man may be unable to do so. If this be a hardship and an inequality, then, it belongs not to this law, but grows out of the state of society, and is involved in the administration of all laws. The poor man cannot command the services of eminent counsel as the rich one can; but is this a good reason why he should not be tried for the offences he may commit? This misfortune of poverty, the Maine law will lift, as a heavy burden, from the shoulders of the poor; and it is, therefore, emphatically, the poor man's friend. And hence I invoke the poor, by every motive of self-interest as well as of duty, to unite in introducing a great public blessing, of which more than a common share will be their own.

Under the auspices of this beneficent law, I trust the time has now come, when the importer of intoxicating liquors will discover some other stream of wealth than that which flows to him from ten thousand fountains of sorrow; when the distiller will no longer seek to get his fine gold by casting human hearts into fires hotter than those of his own caldrons; and when the wealthy owners of real estate will feel that they are abetters and accomplices in the guilt of this inhuman traffic, so long as they derive revenues from marts where men exchange health for disease, reason for insanity, innocence for remorse, and happiness and length of days for misery and an ignominious death. In the promise and prospect of the healing of millions of wretched hearts, there is a foretaste of divine and eternal joy which must enkindle the fervor and combine the energies of all men who ask for themselves a respectable name and place in society.

It is too plain for argument, that the suppression of intemperance is a preliminary process in every social amelioration. What useful or desirable end can ever be subserved by the intemperate? Will they help to advance the progress of any science, of any kind of art or literature, or to promote a single rational pleasure or comfort of any man's life? Would not the United States be a far richer and a far happier nation, if the four hundred thousand drunkards it is said to contain were to be laid in their graves before another setting sun? And what a heaven of blessedness to them and to all it would usher in, were they to be visited by the angel of reformation instead of the angel of death! What can Bible or Christianizing Societies do with the intemperate? At best, they can only address moral and religious sentiments whose animation is suspended. All the Benevolent Associations formed for the relief of orphans and widows, and for clothing, feeding, and educating the children of the intemperate poor, have no resources commensurate with the victims of orphanage, widowhood, and penury, whom intemperance is constantly throwing upon their hands. And how can the patriot forefend the evils which the suffrages of intemperate men will inflict upon his country? We know that, on all moral and social questions, this class of men is prone to vote for the retrogradation of society; and to attempt to prevent it, while they remain intemperate, is like an attempt to stop ocean tides with a bulrush. Let, then, every man who feels himself connected with the human race by any tie of interest, pride, honor, patriotism, philanthropy, or religion, join in one sovereign effort to cast from mankind this mountain weight of iniquity. In an especial manner, let the prosperous and the gifted, — the favored of fortune in their ample stores, and the beloved of nature in their lofty endowments, — fulfil the great mission of beneficence to which they have been appointed, — their superior gifts being their charter. Let them embrace the inspiring idea of leaving the world better than they found it, and of giving scope to the sublime law of Human Progression. Let the good and the great, wherever found, send abroad thoughts and words of electric power, till the nation shall be roused from its lethargy, and the awakened earth shall shake itself free from this unnatural thraldom. Nowhere can the lovers of their kind discover a nobler field for benevolent exertion. In no other theme can the Christian orator find arguments of such resistless power to awaken the dormant, or to overawe and reclaim the wicked. Nor is there aught in the enchantments of immortal verse like the uplifting music of the song with which the ransomed captive celebrates his deliverance from guilty bondage.

I invoke the sons of genius, through the sure promotion and supremacy of this cause, to add a lustre to their names which the highest perfection of their own beautiful arts can never give, and which no corrosions of time can ever impair. Painters! Sculptors! representatives of a race whose eldest born dwelt amid forms of eternal beauty, and whose hallowed spirits, in every age, have presided over the sanctuaries where genius has worshipped; know you not that there are forms of loftier beauty than any which ever shone in the galleries of art; — souls! souls, created in the very likeness of God! but now faded, blackened, defiled, deformed, — yet still capable of renovation, still capable of being apparelled in such celestial coloring, and of bearing such a divine impress as no skill of human artist can ever emulate! I know that the out-raying gladness of the forms which quicken beneath your plastic skill betoken to the eye of sense a living spirit within; yet reason assures us that, though we call them "divine," they are still unconscious.

They are not happy, nor can you breathe into them the Promethean fire. However deeply they may thrill or ravish us, we know their charms are external only; that no immortal spirit is enshrined beneath their surface; that conscience, benevolence, and joy are not their attributes. Spare, then, a brief hour, to shed actual blessedness on bosoms whose heavings and anguish are no illusion of the senses. Leave, for a time, the dead marble and the insensate canvas; mount up to higher conceptions of art than to give coloring, however brilliant, or shape, however exquisite, to inanimate forms; go from perishable matter to the imperishable spirit, and pour blissful feelings deep-inward, along the agonized nerve and the quivering heartstrings. You shape the semblance of divinest contour and features, but they are cold and motionless; their very existence to themselves is death, and day and night are alike darkness to them; — is it not nobler to waken, all the day long, in redeemed households, such spontaneous songs of joy as the statue of Memnon never uttered, and to send dreams of paradise, by night, to visit the once thorny pillow of wife and children? Rise, then, from the feigned to the real, and by reluming the human countenance with the light of long-departed joys, convert your own loveliest emblems into glorious realities. As you await a happy moment of inspiration to give the last, lighting-up touches to your own choicest works; so seize the higher inspirations of benevolence to solace the disconsolate, and thus give a hallowing finish, an unfading halo, to your own fame, and consecrate the immortality you win.

Ministers! Evangelists! you, who claim to be messengers of peace on earth, and heralds of glad tidings to men; you, to whom are given the motives of two worlds to guide the conduct of one! Are not all the truths, whether of time or of eternity, your willing auxiliaries in this cause; and, with heavenly combatants, can you not subdue an earth-born foe? Until this great crime is exterminated, your divine work is scarcely begun. Rocks of adamant will heed your mission sooner than the rebel heart of intemperance. The former are passive, the latter is aggressively hostile. Intemperance goes before you, sterilizing the earth. It follows your footsteps, uprooting whatever you may have transplanted from heaven. It seduces the unconscious young into guilty beginnings. It stands at every crossing in the highways of life, and points the unwary the road to death. All who are enthralled by its power, it corrupts, maddens, demonizes; and every day, while you are delaying, it gathers new strength, and meditates bolder rebellions against the Most High. So far as you do not vanquish this enemy, you and your cause are vanquished. Hasten, then, to the work of reform. Be disquieted and inconsolable. Sorrow for an erring brother will supply the energy to reclaim him. Admonish, persuade, supplicate, in words of wisdom, and in the spirit of an all-comprehending sympathy. Remember that love is a universal solvent, and that wise actions are prayers which Heaven always answers. Rest not, cease not, until every captive is unbound; until, within your several spheres of action, there shall not be one father whose gray hairs are brought down with sorrow to the grave by an intemperate son; nor one son who shall not be able to say, in language as touching as that of the parable, My *father* was dead, and is alive again, was lost,.but is found.

I invoke also the loveliness and the energies of Woman for this holy work. Let her pour her tenderest pathos into the ears of men until the hardness of their hearts shall be melted away. Let mothers and sisters combine, and create a social power more formidable and pervasive than the ballot, — a power that shall reach the spreaders of human ruin, not only on election days, but on all days; and baffle not only their political ambitions and hopes, but all their ambitions and hopes, until they shall abstain from so mighty a wrong. As a Sister of Charity, woman has so long sought, with unavailing effort, to succor the multitudinous victims of intemperance, that we wonder that ere this she has not turned Gorgon, to avenge the woes which have proved too manifold and deep for mortal sympathy to compass or to console. In the natural world, there is a law of storms, which directs their course, and determines the point of their direst intensity. The more desolating tempests of this vice have also their law; and it is, that wherever the wife and the mother may be, there is always the centre of the storm; there its rage beats fiercest, and its howlings are most terrific.

Young men, — you last, you chiefest, let me implore! You, whose precious privilege it still is, to make life long by commencing the performance of its duties early! Where lie your own welfare, your own honor, your own blessedness? Lie they not in that future course of life which is to flow out of your own minds and hearts, and which your own hands are to fashion, as the temple is fashioned by the builder? *The Future*, that greatest heritage on earth, is all your own. Dilate, expand your thoughts to some comprehension of its value. Each day is a tablet which is put into your hands, unmarked by a single line. Your thoughts, your resolves, your deeds, for that day, are engraven upon it; it is then taken away and deposited in the chambers of the indestructible Past. There, by an irreversible law of God, it must remain forever; nor time, nor decay, nor man, nor angels can ever obliterate a word of its eternal record. Let that record be your glory, and not your shame, forever. You have the ladder that Jacob only dreamed of.

When a Roman youth passed from minority to manhood,—when he ceased to be a child in the family, and became a pillar of the state,—the day of his emancipation was celebrated with solemn services. The ceremony of putting on the graceful garment of manhood, in token that the duties of manhood were then to be assumed, was performed on some great festival day of the nation, amid crowds of assembled friends, and under the auspices of his household gods. Thence, in long procession, they moved to some public temple, where, with songs and vows, they implored the divinities to crown with honor and usefulness the life of the new-born citizen; while he himself was commended, and, as it were, apprenticed, to the example of some of the city's illustrious men. Such were the solemn rites and aspirations which ushered a young man into life in pagan Rome. What holy resolutions, then, what self-consecration of the entire life to truth and duty, befit the aspiring and ingenuous youth of the American republic! As your fathers are swiftly passing away into the realms of silence, do not all the transcendent interests of society, its prosperity, its happiness, its honor in distant lands and in distant times, devolve upon you? How is all that is precious in our public institutions to be ennobled, and transmitted, from early ancestors to late posterity, unless one generation after another shall receive and improve, and then pass it onward, as from hand to hand? Grasp, then, this conception of your high destiny. Embody it in deeds. Your power to fulfil it is the choicest boon of Heaven; and ere the habits, the morals, the institutions of society pass beyond your reach forever, redeem them from all pollution, cast out from them the seeds of death and every element of decay, and imbue them with the immortal strength of knowledge, purity, and Temperance.

www.ingramcontent.com/pod-product-compliance
Lightning Source LLC
LaVergne TN
LVHW021420110826
845150LV00007B/2014